THE FEMININE DIVINE

HONORING THE GODDESSES OF INDIA

DR. MINAKSHI BANSAL

Made with ♥ on the Notion Press Platform
www.notionpress.com

DEDICATION

To the goddesses who have inspired this journey, and to the women everywhere who embody their strength, wisdom, and compassion. This book is dedicated to my mother, whose unwavering faith and devotion have been a guiding light in my life, and to all the mothers, daughters, sisters, and friends who carry the divine feminine within them. May the stories and teachings of these revered goddesses inspire and uplift you, and may you always find strength and solace in their timeless wisdom.

ᰔᰔᰔ

Contents

Contents

Prayer

"Om Bhadram Karnebhih Shrinuyama Devah

Bhadram Pashyemakshabhiryajatrah

Sthirairangais Tushtuvamsastanubhih

Vyashema Devahitam Yadayuh

Svasti Na Indro Vriddhashravah

Svasti Nah Pusha Vishwavedah

Svasti Nastarkshyo Arishtanemih

Svasti No Brihaspatir Dadhatu

Om Shantih Shantih Shantih"

This mantra is a prayer for universal well-being, invoking the blessings of various deities for protection, health, and happiness. It emphasizes the importance of experiencing the auspicious through all senses and living a life aligned with divine purpose. The repetition of "Shantih" at the end signifies a deep desire for peace in the individual, the environment, and the universe at large. This mantra is often recited as a prayer for peace, prosperity, and the physical and spiritual well-being of all beings.

ﭯﭯﭯ

About The Author

This book represents the culmination of extensive research and meticulous analysis, incorporating a diverse range of sources, including numerous books, scholarly studies, and personal experiences. Additionally, I have scoured various websites to gather relevant information and data essential for the compilation of this work. I have taken every precaution to ensure the accuracy of the information presented and have diligently cited all sources to acknowledge their contributions.

From her earliest days, Minakshi was distinguished by an insatiable appetite for reading. Her literary universe was inhabited by characters and narratives that spanned ethical tales, motivational and inspirational stories, and the mythic parables imbued with life lessons. This voracious reading habit was not merely for personal edification but was driven by a desire to distill and disseminate the essence of these narratives to foster the development of students and peers alike. She was particularly captivated by the lives and teachings of historical figures and spiritual leaders such as Adi Shankaracharya, Swami Vivekananda, Dr. APJ Abdul Kalam, Mahamana Pandit Madan Mohan Malviya, Mahatma Gandhi, Sardar Vallabhai Patel, and Vinoba Bhave, among others. Their philosophies and life stories fueled her ambition to embody their ideals of resilience, selflessness, and relentless pursuit of knowledge.

Dr. Minakshi's academic and practical engagement with psychology has been equally noteworthy. As a research scholar, her focus has been on exploring the intricate tapestry of the human psyche, aiming to unlock the potential for psychological well-being and societal harmony. Her scholarly work is complemented by her active involvement in social work, where she employs her academic insights to make tangible differences in the lives of the underprivileged. Her endeavours in social work are characterized by an innovative approach that combines traditional wisdom with contemporary psychological practices to address the multifaceted challenges faced by these communities.

Her artistic talents, another facet of her diverse capabilities, are not merely a personal passion but also serve as a medium through which she communicates and connects with others. Her art, rich in symbolism and emotional depth, reflects her philosophical inquiries and social concerns, offering viewers a glimpse into the breadth of her intellect and the depth of her compassion.

In addition to her contributions to the arts and social sciences, Dr. Minakshi has embraced the healing arts of Pranic Healing, mastering the techniques developed by Master Choa Kok Sui. This practice, which focuses on the manipulation of Prana or life energy to heal the body and aura, has been both a personal journey of discovery and a means through which she extends her healing touch to others. Her proficiency in Pranic Healing is complemented by her advocacy and teaching of various forms of meditation aimed at rejuvenation, personal betterment, and the cultivation of harmony within individuals and communities alike.

Dr. Minakshi's life is a narrative of relentless pursuit, not just of personal achievement but of the upliftment and empowerment of society at large. Her diverse interests and talents—spanning the arts, literature, psychology, and the healing practices—converge on a singular path of service. She embodies the spirit of the luminaries who inspired her, channelling their legacy through her actions and teachings. Through her books, art, and social initiatives, she continues to inspire a new generation to embark on their own journeys of self-discovery, resilience, and altruism.

Her commitment to social betterment, particularly her focus on uplifting underprivileged children, reflects a deep understanding of the transformative potential of education and personal development. By integrating her knowledge of psychology, her artistic sensibilities, and her healing practices, Dr. Bansal has developed a holistic approach to social work that addresses both the immediate needs and the long-term well-being of the communities she serves.

As an author, Dr. Minakshi's writings offer a blend of inspirational insights, practical wisdom, and reflective contemplations drawn from her extensive reading and life experiences. Her books serve as a guide for those seeking to navigate the complexities of life with grace, resilience, and purpose. Through her narratives, she extends an invitation to her readers to explore the depths of their own potential and to contribute meaningfully to the collective well-being of society.

In Dr. Minakshi Bansal, we find a remarkable synthesis of the artist, the scholar, the healer, and the social activist. Her life's work stands as a beacon of hope and a source of inspiration for individuals seeking to make a difference in the world. Her story is a compelling reminder of the power of individual action, rooted in compassion and driven by a profound commitment to the betterment of humanity. Dr. Minakshi's legacy is not just in the tangible outcomes of her efforts but in the enduring spirit of inquiry, empathy, and service that she embodies.

ppp

Preface

The inspiration for this book emerged from a profound desire to explore and celebrate the multifaceted manifestations of the divine feminine in Hindu mythology. Growing up in a culture steeped in the rich traditions of Indian spirituality, I was always captivated by the stories of goddesses who embody strength, compassion, wisdom, and resilience. These goddesses, with their diverse attributes and powerful narratives, offer a wealth of spiritual and cultural insights that are as relevant today as they were in ancient times. This book is a tribute to their enduring presence and significance in the lives of millions of devotees.

From a young age, I was drawn to the sacred tales and hymns that extolled the virtues of these divine figures. The festivals, rituals, and daily practices that honored these goddesses were not just religious observances but a vital part of community life, reflecting the deep reverence and devotion that permeate Indian culture. As I delved deeper into these stories, I began to see how they transcend mere mythology, offering profound lessons on navigating the complexities of life with grace, strength, and wisdom. These goddesses are not distant, abstract figures; they are intimately connected to the natural world and the human experience, embodying qualities and principles that resonate with our innermost aspirations and challenges.

In writing this book, I sought to capture the essence of these goddesses and their teachings, drawing on a wide range of sources, including ancient scriptures, devotional literature, and contemporary interpretations. Each goddess represents a unique aspect of the divine feminine, and their stories are rich with symbolism and meaning. By exploring their narratives, iconography, and cultural significance, I aim to provide a comprehensive and accessible guide to understanding their roles and relevance in both historical and modern contexts.

The process of researching and writing this book has been a deeply enriching journey, one that has deepened my appreciation for the intricate tapestry of Indian spirituality. The goddesses I have written about are more than just subjects of academic interest; they are living presences that continue to inspire and guide individuals and communities across the world. Through their worship and veneration, devotees find strength, solace, and a sense of connection to something greater than themselves. This book is an offering to those who seek to deepen their understanding of these divine figures and their timeless teachings.

One of the most striking aspects of the goddesses of India is their embodiment of both nurturing and fierce qualities. They are mothers, warriors, healers, and protectors, each bringing their unique energies to the cosmic balance. This duality is a reflection of the holistic understanding of the feminine in Indian spirituality, which encompasses creation, preservation, and destruction. The stories of these goddesses challenge the often simplistic and reductive notions of femininity, presenting a vision of the feminine as powerful, dynamic, and integral to the fabric of existence.

The goddess Lalita Tripura Sundari, for instance, is revered as the epitome of beauty, grace, and bliss. Her worship, rooted in the Tantric traditions, emphasizes the pursuit of spiritual enlightenment and the realization of one's unity with the divine. Through her thousand names, Lalita is celebrated as the universal mother, the source of all creation, and the embodiment of compassion. Her teachings inspire devotees to cultivate inner beauty and grace, transcending the material illusions that often cloud our perception of reality.

Vindhyavasini, the mountain-dwelling goddess, embodies the strength and resilience of the natural world. Her association with the Vindhya Range highlights the deep connection between the divine and the environment. Vindhyavasini's role as a protector and warrior underscores the importance of courage and determination in the face of adversity. Her worship reflects a profound respect for nature and the understanding that the natural world is imbued with divine energy.

Tulsi, the sacred plant and divine Devi, represents the integration of spirituality and everyday life. Revered as a manifestation of Lakshmi, Tulsi is both a sacred plant and a symbol of devotion and purity. Her presence in households and her use in Ayurvedic medicine highlight the holistic approach to health and well-being that is central to Indian spirituality. The rituals and festivals dedicated to Tulsi emphasize the importance of living in harmony with nature and recognizing the divine in the natural world.

Gayatri, the personification of the Vedic hymn, embodies the pursuit of knowledge and enlightenment. The Gayatri Mantra, one of the most powerful and revered hymns in Hinduism, is a prayer for spiritual awakening and the illumination of the intellect. Gayatri's teachings promote the values of intellectual and spiritual growth, encouraging devotees to seek wisdom and align their lives with the higher principles of truth and righteousness.

Bhumi, the Earth Goddess, represents the nurturing and sustaining aspects of the Earth. As the personification of the planet, Bhumi embodies qualities of fertility, stability, and nourishment. Her worship underscores the intimate relationship between humans and the Earth, emphasizing the need for ecological stewardship and respect for the environment. Bhumi's significance extends to various cultural and literary traditions, where she is celebrated as a symbol of resilience and the interconnectedness of all life.

Manasa, the serpent goddess of fertility and health, highlights the protective and healing aspects of the divine feminine. Revered for her ability to cure snakebites and promote fertility, Manasa's worship reflects a deep connection to the natural world and the cycles of life. Her story, celebrated in the Manasa Mangal, emphasizes the virtues of resilience, devotion, and compassion. Manasa's teachings remind us of the importance of respecting and protecting the natural world and its creatures.

Santoshi Mata, the Mother of Satisfaction, is a relatively recent addition to the Hindu pantheon, yet her worship has quickly gained prominence. Known for her ability to grant peace and contentment, Santoshi Mata's teachings emphasize the values of patience, perseverance, and devotion. The rituals associated with her worship, such as the Santoshi Mata Vrat, highlight the importance of faith and the pursuit of harmony in familial and personal life.

Kamakhya, the goddess of desire and fertility, is a central figure in the tantric practices of Assam. Her worship, centered around the Kamakhya Temple, celebrates the sacredness of desire and the feminine body. The Ambubachi Mela, a festival marking Kamakhya's menstruation, underscores her role as a goddess of fertility and the life-giving properties of the Earth. Kamakhya's teachings emphasize the acceptance and transcendence of physical desires as a path to spiritual enlightenment.

Chandi, the fierce form of Shakti, embodies the protective and transformative aspects of the divine feminine. Her story, recounted in the Devi Mahatmya, celebrates her might and valor in battling the forces of darkness. Chandi's teachings promote the values of courage, resilience, and the importance of confronting and overcoming adversity. Her worship, particularly during Durga Puja, reflects her significance as a warrior goddess and protector of the cosmos.

Radha, the symbol of divine love, is celebrated for her pure and selfless love for Krishna. Her relationship with Krishna represents the soul's yearning for union with the divine. The stories of Radha and Krishna, filled with enchanting episodes of their divine play in Vrindavan, highlight the intensity and spiritual depth of their love. Radha's devotion to Krishna is marked by intense longing and separation, symbolizing the soul's journey towards spiritual enlightenment. Her worship emphasizes the values of love, devotion, and spiritual union.

Sita, the embodiment of virtue and devotion, is one of the most revered figures in Hindu mythology. As the consort of Lord Rama, Sita exemplifies the ideals of righteousness and devotion. Her life, marked by trials and tribulations, reflects the virtues of patience, purity, and unwavering dedication to dharma. Sita's story, chronicled in the Ramayana, provides profound insights into the ideals of dharma and the transformative power of devotion. Her unwavering faith, moral integrity, and compassionate nature make her an enduring figure of inspiration and reverence.

Parvati, the gentle mother and nurturer, stands as a symbol of love, devotion, and compassion. As the consort of Lord Shiva and the mother of Ganesha and Kartikeya, Parvati embodies the ideal qualities of womanhood. Her life story, filled with devotion and perseverance, highlights her role as a nurturing and protective mother. Parvati's teachings emphasize the importance of balance, perseverance, and compassion, encouraging individuals to cultivate virtues such as love and resilience.

Kali, the fierce protector and destroyer, represents the darker and more powerful aspects of the divine feminine. As a manifestation of Parvati, Kali embodies the destructive and transformative forces necessary to maintain cosmic balance. Her fearsome appearance, with wild hair, a garland of skulls, and a protruding tongue, symbolizes the raw and untamed energy of the divine. Kali's teachings emphasize the importance of embracing one's shadow self and the transformative power of facing fears and challenges.

Her worship, particularly during festivals like Kali Puja, reflects her role as a protector against evil and a guide through the darker aspects of existence.

Saraswati, the goddess of wisdom and learning, is revered as the embodiment of knowledge, music, and the arts. She is often depicted holding a veena and a book, symbolizing the integration of artistic and intellectual pursuits. Saraswati's teachings encourage the development of intellectual and artistic talents, promoting the values of learning and cultural enrichment. Her worship, especially during the festival of Vasant Panchami, highlights the importance of education, creativity, and the pursuit of knowledge.

Lakshmi, the bestower of wealth and prosperity, is one of the most widely worshipped goddesses in Hinduism. As the consort of Vishnu, Lakshmi embodies the qualities of abundance, fortune, and beauty. Her presence in households and businesses reflects the desire for prosperity and well-being. The festival of Diwali, dedicated to Lakshmi, is a time for invoking her blessings for wealth and success. Lakshmi's teachings emphasize the importance of gratitude, generosity, and ethical living in the pursuit of prosperity.

Dr. Minakshi Bansal
Social Activist
Ahmedabad, Gujarat, Bharat

ppp

ONE

THE ESSENCE OF SHAKTI: UNDERSTANDING THE FEMININE POWER

The concept of Shakti, which means "power" or "energy" in Sanskrit, is one of the most profound and essential aspects of Hindu philosophy. It represents the dynamic forces that are thought to move through the entire universe. Understanding Shakti is crucial to grasping the essence of feminine power in Hinduism. This principle is not merely a metaphor but a vital force that embodies the feminine aspect of divinity and existence itself.

Shakti is often personified as a goddess and revered as the Supreme Being. She is the mother of the universe, the life force that pervades everything and is responsible for creation, preservation, and destruction. In Hindu mythology, Shakti is often seen as the consort of the major male gods, such as Shiva, Vishnu, and Brahma, and she manifests in various forms and names, including Durga, Kali, Parvati, Lakshmi, and Saraswati. Each of these goddesses represents different aspects of the same divine power, demonstrating the multifaceted nature of feminine energy.

The story of Shakti begins with the primordial cosmic energy that existed before time and space. According to Hindu cosmology, the universe is cyclically created and destroyed, and it is Shakti who plays a crucial role in these processes. She is both the creative force that brings the universe into existence and the destructive power that dissolves it back into chaos, making way for new creation. This cyclical nature of creation and destruction highlights the essential role of Shakti in maintaining the balance of the cosmos.

One of the most important aspects of Shakti is her role as the creative force. In this context, she is often associated with Prakriti, the material world, and is seen as the source of all life and existence. The universe is born out of her womb, and she nurtures and sustains it. This creative power is not limited to the physical realm but also extends to the intellectual and spiritual dimensions. Shakti is the inspiration behind all forms of art, music, and literature, as well as the wisdom and knowledge that guide human civilization. This aspect of Shakti is particularly embodied by the goddess Saraswati, who is worshipped as the goddess of learning and the arts.

Shakti's role as a preserver is equally significant. In this aspect, she is often associated with the goddess Lakshmi, who is the consort of Vishnu, the preserver god in Hinduism. Lakshmi represents wealth, prosperity, and well-being. She ensures that life is sustained and nurtured, providing the resources and blessings needed for growth and development. Through her, Shakti manifests as the sustaining power that maintains the order and harmony of the universe, allowing it to thrive and flourish.

The destructive aspect of Shakti is perhaps the most misunderstood. It is not destruction for the sake of chaos but a necessary process that clears the way for new creation. This is vividly represented by the goddess Kali, who is often depicted with a fierce and terrifying countenance. Kali's role as the destroyer is to eliminate evil and ignorance, making way for the light of knowledge and righteousness. She embodies the transformative power of Shakti, which is essential for spiritual growth and enlightenment. Without destruction, there can be no renewal, and Kali's fierce love ensures that the cycle of life continues unabated.

Another vital dimension of Shakti is her role as the mother and nurturer. In this aspect, she is most commonly associated with the goddess Parvati, the consort of Shiva. Parvati represents the gentle and nurturing side of Shakti, the loving mother who cares for her children and the devoted wife who supports her husband. This nurturing aspect is not limited to familial relationships but extends to all of creation. Shakti, as the mother of the universe, cares for all beings, providing them with the love and support they need to grow and evolve.

Shakti is also seen as a powerful warrior who fights to protect the righteous and uphold justice. This warrior aspect is most famously embodied by the goddess Durga, who is often depicted riding a lion and wielding various weapons. Durga's battles against demons and evil forces symbolize the eternal struggle between good and evil, light and darkness. Her victories remind devotees that divine feminine power is always available to overcome obstacles and defeat negative forces, both within and outside ourselves.

The worship of Shakti is a central part of Hindu religious practice. Festivals such as Navratri, which celebrates the nine forms of Shakti, are observed with great devotion and enthusiasm. These celebrations highlight the various aspects of the goddess and encourage devotees to seek her blessings for strength, wisdom, prosperity, and protection. Through rituals, prayers, and offerings, followers connect with the divine feminine energy and invite it into their lives.

Understanding Shakti also involves recognizing the balance and harmony between the masculine and feminine principles. In Hindu philosophy, the universe is sustained by the interplay between these two forces. The masculine principle, often personified by gods like Shiva, Vishnu, and Brahma, represents consciousness, stability, and order. In contrast, the feminine principle, represented by Shakti, embodies energy, dynamism, and change. It is the dance between these two forces that creates and sustains the universe. This interplay is beautifully depicted in the concept of Ardhanarishvara, a composite form of Shiva and Parvati, symbolizing the inseparable nature of masculine and feminine energies.

The principle of Shakti extends beyond mythology and religious practice; it has profound implications for the social and cultural roles of women. In many ways, the reverence for Shakti reflects the high regard for feminine power and its vital role in society. Women, seen as embodiments of Shakti, are honored and respected for their creative, nurturing, and transformative abilities. This respect is evident in various cultural practices, traditions, and social structures that celebrate and empower women.

However, it is also essential to recognize that the concept of Shakti challenges and transcends traditional gender roles. Shakti is not confined to women; it is a universal force that exists within all beings, regardless of gender. Everyone possesses a balance of masculine and feminine energies, and understanding Shakti involves embracing this inner duality. By acknowledging and cultivating both aspects of our nature, we can achieve greater harmony and fulfillment in our lives.

In modern times, the essence of Shakti continues to inspire

movements for gender equality and women's empowerment. The recognition of feminine power as a vital and sacred force challenges patriarchal structures and calls for a more balanced and inclusive approach to social and cultural issues. Women drawing upon the strength and resilience of Shakti are at the forefront of efforts to create a more just and equitable world.

The essence of Shakti, therefore, is a celebration of the feminine power that is intrinsic to all life. It is a recognition of the dynamic and multifaceted nature of the divine feminine, encompassing creation, preservation, destruction, nurturing, and protection. Through the worship and understanding of Shakti, devotees connect with the fundamental energy that drives the universe and gain insight into their own inner strength and potential.

In understanding Shakti, we come to appreciate the profound and intricate balance of forces that sustain the cosmos. The recognition of this balance invites us to embrace the diverse and dynamic aspects of our own nature, fostering a deeper connection with the world around us and the divine within. Shakti's essence is a reminder that true power lies not in domination but in the harmonious interplay of energies, the creative force of life, and the nurturing love that sustains us all.

By honoring Shakti, we honor the feminine power within ourselves and the universe, acknowledging its essential role in the dance of existence. This understanding opens the door to a more holistic and integrated approach to spirituality, one that celebrates the beauty and strength of the divine feminine and its indispensable contribution to the unfolding story of life.

ॐॐॐ

"The goddesses of Hindu mythology embody the divine feminine's strength, wisdom, and compassion. They guide us through life's challenges with grace and resilience. Their stories are timeless lessons in navigating the complexities of existence."

TWO
DURGA: THE INVINCIBLE WARRIOR GODDESS

Durga, the invincible warrior goddess, stands as one of the most revered and powerful deities in Hindu mythology. Her story is one of valor, strength, and compassion, embodying the quintessential essence of feminine power. Durga's tale is not just a mythological narrative but a profound spiritual and philosophical symbol that resonates with the eternal struggle between good and evil, righteousness and malevolence, and light and darkness. She represents the divine energy that protects the cosmos and restores balance whenever it is threatened.

Durga's origin is rooted in a cosmic crisis. According to Hindu mythology, the world was once terrorized by the demon Mahishasura, a formidable adversary who possessed the power to shape-shift between a buffalo and a human. Mahishasura, through severe penance, had acquired a boon from the god Brahma, which made him invincible against any man or god. Drunk with power and arrogance, he unleashed a reign of terror, subjugating gods and humans alike, plunging the universe into chaos and despair. The gods, unable to defeat Mahishasura, sought the help of the supreme trinity – Brahma, Vishnu, and Shiva.

In response to the prayers and pleas of the gods, the supreme trinity combined their energies to create a powerful goddess. From their collective energies emerged Durga, radiant and majestic, with a countenance that exuded both serenity and strength. Each god bestowed upon her their most potent weapons – Shiva gave her his trident, Vishnu his discus, Varuna his conch, Agni his spear, Vayu his bow and arrows, Indra his thunderbolt, and so forth. Mounted on a lion, Durga epitomized divine power and determination, ready to confront and vanquish the demonic forces threatening cosmic balance.

Durga's battle with Mahishasura is one of the most epic tales in Hindu mythology. It is recounted in the Devi Mahatmya, a text that forms part of the Markandeya Purana. For nine days and nights, Durga fought Mahishasura and his army, displaying unparalleled strength, skill, and bravery. Each encounter with the demon showcased her martial prowess and strategic acumen. Mahishasura's shape-shifting abilities posed a significant challenge, but Durga, unyielding and resolute, adapted to his every move. The battle culminated on the tenth day when Durga, with her trident, pierced Mahishasura's heart, ending his tyranny and restoring peace and order to the universe. This victory is celebrated annually as Vijayadashami or Dussehra, a festival that signifies the triumph of good over evil.

Durga's iconography is rich with symbolism that encapsulates her role as the invincible warrior goddess. She is often depicted with multiple arms, each holding a weapon, symbolizing her ability to combat numerous threats simultaneously. Her lion mount represents courage and strength, while her serene face amidst the ferocity of battle signifies her divine composure and grace. The weapons she wields are not just instruments of war but symbols of various virtues and powers: the trident represents the power to destroy evil; the discus symbolizes the cyclical nature of time and righteousness; the conch embodies the primal sound of creation and the dissemination of knowledge; the bow and arrows signify focused energy and direction; and the thunderbolt represents the indomitable spirit and the capacity to annihilate ignorance.

Durga's narrative transcends her martial exploits and delves into deeper spiritual and philosophical dimensions. She is not just a warrior but a mother, a nurturer, and a protector. Her maternal aspect is often highlighted in her epithet "Durga Ma" or "Mother Durga." She is the compassionate mother who fiercely protects her children from harm and guides them towards righteousness. This duality of being both a fierce warrior and a loving mother reflects the complex and holistic nature of the divine feminine. It underscores the idea that true strength lies not just in the ability to fight but also in the capacity to nurture and care.

The worship of Durga is a central aspect of Hindu religious practice, particularly during the festival of Navratri, which spans nine nights and culminates in Vijayadashami. During Navratri, devotees engage in fasting, prayer, and various rituals to honor the nine forms of Durga, collectively known as Navadurga. Each form represents a different aspect of the goddess and her divine qualities. The festival is a time of spiritual reflection, renewal, and celebration, emphasizing the victory of light over darkness and the power of the divine feminine.

Durga's influence extends beyond religious worship and into cultural and social spheres. She is a symbol of empowerment, particularly for women. In a society where women have often been subjected to oppression and inequality, Durga stands as a beacon of strength and resilience. Her story inspires women to rise above challenges, assert their power, and fight against injustice. The imagery of Durga as a warrior goddess has been a powerful motif in various movements for women's rights and empowerment in India and beyond. She embodies the idea that femininity and strength are not mutually exclusive but are, in fact, intrinsically connected.

The philosophical underpinnings of Durga's narrative also offer profound insights into the nature of good and evil. Mahishasura, the demon, represents the ego and the darker aspects of the human psyche – arrogance, ignorance, and unchecked desire. Durga's battle against Mahishasura symbolizes the inner struggle that each individual must undertake to overcome these negative tendencies and achieve spiritual enlightenment. Her victory is a reminder that divine grace and inner strength can conquer even the most formidable adversaries. This allegorical interpretation of Durga's story provides a timeless and universal message about the triumph of the higher self over the baser instincts.

Durga's relevance in contemporary times is particularly poignant. In an era marked by social, political, and environmental turmoil, her narrative serves as a powerful reminder of the need for courage, resilience, and righteous action. The values she embodies – strength, compassion, justice, and wisdom – are more pertinent than ever. Her story encourages individuals and societies to confront their challenges head-on, to fight against injustice, and to strive for a harmonious and balanced existence.

Furthermore, Durga's iconography and symbolism have been adapted and reinterpreted in various artistic and cultural expressions. From classical dance forms like Bharatanatyam and Kathak, which depict episodes from her life, to contemporary art and literature, Durga continues to inspire creativity and innovation. Her imagery is a common motif in Indian art, appearing in paintings, sculptures, and temple architecture, reflecting her enduring presence in the cultural consciousness.

The theological significance of Durga is also profound. She is often identified with the concept of Brahman, the ultimate reality in Hindu philosophy. In the Advaita Vedanta tradition, Durga is seen as the dynamic aspect of Brahman, the force that animates and sustains the universe. This identification with the ultimate reality elevates her status beyond that of a deity to that of the fundamental principle of existence. Her worship is thus not just a ritualistic practice but a means of connecting with the divine essence that pervades all of creation.

In understanding Durga, it is essential to appreciate the rich tapestry of myths, symbols, and philosophies that surround her. She is a multifaceted deity who transcends simple categorization. Her narrative is a confluence of mythological, spiritual, and cultural elements that together create a compelling and inspiring figure. Durga's story is a testament to the enduring power of myth and its ability to convey profound truths about the human experience.

Durga, the invincible warrior goddess, remains a central figure in the Hindu pantheon and a powerful symbol of the divine feminine. Her story, rich in symbolism and spiritual significance, offers timeless lessons about strength, resilience, and the eternal struggle between good and evil. As both a warrior and a mother, she embodies the complex and holistic nature of feminine power, inspiring devotion and reverence among her followers. Her influence extends beyond religious worship, permeating cultural and social spheres, and serving as a beacon of empowerment and justice. In an ever-changing world, Durga's narrative continues to resonate, reminding us of the enduring power of the divine feminine and its vital role in the cosmic order.

ᎮᎮᎮ

"Lalita Tripura Sundari, the goddess of bliss and beauty, teaches us to seek inner harmony and spiritual enlightenment. Her grace and elegance remind us of the beauty within. Through her, we learn the importance of inner beauty and transcendence."

THREE

LAKSHMI: THE BESTOWER OF WEALTH AND PROSPERITY

Lakshmi, the goddess of wealth and prosperity, holds a central place in Hinduism, embodying the ideals of material and spiritual abundance. Her name is derived from the Sanskrit word "Lakshya," meaning aim or goal, signifying her role as the one who helps devotees achieve their aims and fulfill their desires. As the consort of Vishnu, the preserver of the universe, Lakshmi complements his function by providing the material resources necessary for life and its sustenance. Her influence permeates all aspects of Hindu culture, from daily worship practices to grand festivals, making her an enduring symbol of prosperity and well-being.

The origins of Lakshmi trace back to the Vedic period, where she is first mentioned in the Rigveda as a deity associated with fortune, power, and fertility. Over time, her persona evolved and became more defined in the Puranas and other Hindu scriptures. According to mythology, Lakshmi emerged from the churning of the ocean of milk (Samudra Manthan), a grand event that symbolizes the eternal quest for immortality and the struggle between the gods and demons for the elixir of life.

Her emergence from the ocean, radiant and resplendent, signifies the manifestation of wealth and prosperity from the primal cosmic waters, emphasizing her divine nature and the essential role she plays in the cosmic order.

Lakshmi is often depicted as a beautiful woman with four arms, standing or sitting on a lotus flower. The lotus, a symbol of purity and transcendence, represents spiritual awakening and the unfolding of consciousness. Her four arms denote her omnipresence and power, each holding significant objects: a lotus, symbolizing beauty and fertility; a pot of gold coins, representing material wealth; a conch, indicating the primordial sound and communication; and a discus, signifying the cyclical nature of time and the preservation of righteousness. Sometimes, she is shown with two elephants, Gaja Lakshmi, showering her with water, symbolizing royal power and auspiciousness. The gold coins flowing from her hands signify the constant flow of wealth and prosperity to her devotees.

The worship of Lakshmi is integral to Hindu religious practice, with numerous rituals and festivals dedicated to invoking her blessings. One of the most significant is Diwali, the festival of lights, which celebrates the return of Lord Rama to Ayodhya after his exile and victory over the demon king Ravana. Diwali also commemorates the churning of the ocean and the emergence of Lakshmi.

Devotees clean and decorate their homes, light oil lamps, and offer prayers to Lakshmi, seeking her blessings for wealth, prosperity, and happiness in the coming year. The lighting of lamps signifies the dispelling of ignorance and the illumination of knowledge and wisdom.

Another important festival is Kojagiri Purnima, celebrated on the full moon night of the Ashwin month. It is believed that Lakshmi descends to earth on this night, and those who remain awake and worship her are blessed with wealth and prosperity. Devotees offer special prayers and keep vigil, engaging in devotional singing and reading scriptures dedicated to Lakshmi. The tradition of staying awake signifies vigilance and the readiness to receive the goddess's blessings.

Lakshmi's influence extends beyond material wealth; she also bestows spiritual and moral prosperity. She is associated with the qualities of generosity, kindness, and grace. In her benevolent aspect, she encourages her devotees to cultivate virtues such as charity, humility, and compassion. The story of Sudama, a poor Brahmin and childhood friend of Lord Krishna, illustrates this aspect of Lakshmi's grace. Despite his poverty, Sudama's devotion and humility earned him Krishna's favor, who, with Lakshmi's blessings, transformed his humble hut into a palace, highlighting the idea that true wealth lies in devotion and righteousness.

The philosophical dimension of Lakshmi's worship involves the recognition that material wealth is not an end in itself but a means to achieve higher spiritual goals. In Hinduism, the pursuit of Artha (material wealth) is one of the four Purusharthas, or aims of human life, alongside Dharma (righteousness), Kama (pleasure), and Moksha (liberation).

Lakshmi's blessings are sought not only for personal gain but also for the welfare of society. The wealth bestowed by her should be used for righteous purposes, supporting charitable activities, and contributing to the well-being of others. This perspective underscores the ethical use of wealth and the responsibility that comes with prosperity.

Lakshmi's significance is also evident in her various incarnations and manifestations, each representing different aspects of prosperity and well-being. One of her most well-known incarnations is Sita, the devoted wife of Lord Rama. Sita embodies the virtues of loyalty, purity, and self-sacrifice, highlighting the ideal qualities of womanhood and the importance of moral integrity. Another incarnation is Radha, the beloved of Lord Krishna, symbolizing divine love and devotion. Radha's love for Krishna is seen as the highest form of spiritual longing and union with the divine.

In South India, Lakshmi is worshipped as Andal, a revered poet-saint and the only female Alvar among the twelve Alvar saints of the Tamil Bhakti movement. Andal's devotional poetry, expressing her intense love for Lord Vishnu, is celebrated in the sacred Tamil text, the Divya Prabandham.

Her life and works emphasize the power of devotion and the transformative potential of divine love. Andal's story is a testament to Lakshmi's presence in the cultural and spiritual life of the region, highlighting the universal appeal and significance of the goddess.

Lakshmi's influence is not confined to India but extends to other cultures and religions. In Buddhism, she is known as Vasudhara, the goddess of abundance, fertility, and prosperity. Vasudhara is venerated in Tibetan and Nepalese Buddhism, where she is depicted holding a sheaf of grain, symbolizing agricultural abundance, and a vase overflowing with jewels, representing material wealth. This cross-cultural presence underscores Lakshmi's universal appeal as a symbol of prosperity and well-being.

In Jainism, Lakshmi is associated with the principle of Aishwarya, which signifies wealth and prosperity achieved through righteous means. Jain texts often depict Lakshmi showering wealth on devotees who adhere to the path of Dharma and ethical living. This representation aligns with the broader Jain emphasis on non-violence, ethical conduct, and spiritual purity, reinforcing the idea that true prosperity is attained through moral and righteous actions.

The philosophical teachings associated with Lakshmi also emphasize the transient nature of material wealth and the importance of spiritual wealth. Hindu scriptures, such as the Bhagavad Gita and the Upanishads, often highlight the impermanence of material possessions and the need to seek lasting happiness through spiritual realization. Lakshmi, as the goddess of wealth, serves as a reminder that while material prosperity is necessary for a comfortable life, it is ultimately fleeting and should be balanced with the pursuit of spiritual wisdom and liberation.

Lakshmi's role as the bestower of wealth and prosperity is also reflected in various traditional practices and rituals associated with her worship. One such practice is the installation of the Shree Yantra, a geometric representation of the goddess, in homes and places of worship. The Shree Yantra is believed to attract positive energies and bring prosperity, harmony, and success to the household. Devotees chant mantras and perform rituals to invoke Lakshmi's presence and seek her blessings through the Shree Yantra.

Another common practice is the recitation of the Lakshmi Sahasranama, a hymn that enumerates a thousand names and attributes of the goddess. This recitation is believed to invoke Lakshmi's divine presence and attract her blessings.

Each name of Lakshmi highlights a different aspect of her personality and powers, from her role as the giver of wealth to her embodiment of compassion and grace. The practice of reciting these names serves as a form of meditation and devotion, fostering a deeper connection with the goddess.

Lakshmi's association with wealth and prosperity also extends to various cultural and artistic expressions. In classical Indian dance forms such as Bharatanatyam and Odissi, dancers often depict stories and themes related to Lakshmi through their performances. These dances not only celebrate the goddess's beauty and grace but also convey the deeper spiritual and philosophical messages associated with her worship. Similarly, Indian art and literature abound with representations of Lakshmi, from intricate temple sculptures and paintings to devotional poetry and songs, all reflecting her enduring presence in the cultural imagination.

In contemporary times, Lakshmi continues to be a source of inspiration and guidance for millions of devotees around the world. Her story and symbolism resonate with people from all walks of life, offering solace and hope in times of hardship and uncertainty. The values she embodies – generosity, compassion, and the responsible use of wealth – remain relevant and inspiring, encouraging individuals to strive for a balanced and harmonious life.

Lakshmi's influence also extends to various social and economic initiatives aimed at promoting prosperity and well-being. In rural India, for instance, women's self-help groups often invoke Lakshmi's blessings for their entrepreneurial ventures, seeking her guidance and support in their efforts to achieve financial independence and improve their communities.

These initiatives, rooted in the values of cooperation and mutual support, reflect the broader principles associated with Lakshmi's worship and underscore the goddess's relevance in contemporary efforts to promote economic and social development.

Lakshmi, the bestower of wealth and prosperity, is much more than a deity of material riches. She embodies the principles of abundance, ethical prosperity, and spiritual well-being, guiding her devotees towards a balanced and fulfilling life.

Her presence in Hindu mythology, religious practice, and cultural expressions underscores her enduring significance and universal appeal. Through her blessings, Lakshmi teaches us the true meaning of wealth – one that encompasses material comfort, spiritual wisdom, and moral integrity – and inspires us to pursue a life of righteousness, generosity, and compassion.

ॐॐॐ

"Vindhyavasini, the mountain-dwelling goddess, symbolizes strength and resilience. Her presence in the Vindhya Range reminds us of the power and majesty of nature. She inspires us to face adversity with courage and determination."

FOUR

SARASWATI: THE GODDESS OF WISDOM AND LEARNING

Saraswati, the goddess of wisdom and learning, is one of the most revered deities in Hinduism, symbolizing knowledge, music, art, speech, and learning. She embodies the quintessential ideal of wisdom and is considered the patroness of the arts and sciences. Saraswati's significance extends beyond mere academic knowledge, encompassing the broader spectrum of intellectual and spiritual enlightenment. Her presence is invoked by students, artists, scholars, and musicians alike, seeking her blessings for intellectual clarity, creative inspiration, and eloquent expression.

The origins of Saraswati are deeply rooted in the ancient Vedic tradition. She is first mentioned in the Rigveda, one of the oldest sacred texts of Hinduism, where she is praised as a powerful river goddess and a deity of knowledge and wisdom. Her name, derived from the Sanskrit root "saras," meaning "flow," signifies both her connection to the rivers and the flow of knowledge. Saraswati is often associated with the river Saraswati, a now-mythical river believed to have flowed through the northwestern region of India, which was a cradle of early Vedic civilization. The river symbolized purity, clarity, and the life-sustaining flow of wisdom.

As the Vedic tradition evolved, Saraswati's identity expanded, and she became increasingly associated with intellectual and artistic pursuits. In the later texts, such as the Puranas and the Mahabharata, Saraswati is described as the consort of Brahma, the creator god. She plays a vital role in the process of creation, not only as a divine consort but also as the embodiment of the knowledge and wisdom necessary for creation to occur. Her presence ensures that the act of creation is not just a mechanical process but an enlightened one, imbued with the principles of order, harmony, and beauty.

Saraswati is often depicted as a serene and graceful figure, seated on a white lotus or riding a swan, symbols of purity and transcendence. She is usually shown wearing a white sari, which signifies her purity and her rejection of materialism. In her four arms, she holds a veena (a stringed musical instrument), a book, a mala (prayer beads), and a pot of water. Each of these objects carries profound symbolic meanings: the veena represents the arts, particularly music, and the harmony of creation; the book symbolizes knowledge and learning; the mala signifies meditation and spirituality; and the pot of water represents the purifying power of wisdom. Her swan mount, known for its ability to separate milk from water, symbolizes discernment and the ability to distinguish between truth and falsehood.

The worship of Saraswati is a vital aspect of Hindu religious practice, particularly during the festival of Vasant Panchami, which marks the onset of spring. Vasant Panchami is dedicated to Saraswati, and it is a time when students, artists, and scholars offer prayers and perform rituals to seek her blessings. On this day, educational institutions, from schools to universities, hold special ceremonies to honor Saraswati. Devotees place books, musical instruments, and tools of learning on altars and offer them to the goddess, symbolizing their quest for knowledge and creative inspiration. The festival highlights the importance of education and the pursuit of knowledge in Hindu culture, reinforcing the idea that learning is a sacred and lifelong endeavor.

Saraswati's influence extends beyond formal education and academic pursuits. She is also considered the goddess of eloquence and speech. In Hindu tradition, the power of speech, or Vak, is revered as a divine gift, and Saraswati is seen as its embodiment. The Rigveda extols her as Vakdevi, the goddess of speech, who bestows the gift of articulate and truthful expression. This aspect of Saraswati underscores the belief that words hold power and that the ability to communicate effectively and truthfully is a divine blessing. Poets, writers, and orators invoke Saraswati to guide their words and inspire their creative expression.

In addition to her association with learning and speech, Saraswati is also revered as the goddess of the arts. Music, dance, painting, and other forms of artistic expression are seen as manifestations of her divine energy. The veena, which she holds, is a symbol of the divine melody that permeates the universe, representing the idea that music is a universal language that connects all beings. Saraswati's role as the patroness of the arts emphasizes the integral connection between creativity and spirituality. Artistic expression is viewed not merely as a human endeavor but as a form of divine worship and a means of connecting with the transcendent.

The philosophical dimension of Saraswati's worship involves the recognition that true knowledge encompasses both intellectual understanding and spiritual wisdom. In Hindu thought, knowledge (jnana) is categorized into two types: apara vidya, or lower knowledge, which includes empirical and worldly knowledge; and para vidya, or higher knowledge, which pertains to spiritual understanding and the realization of the self. Saraswati embodies both aspects, guiding her devotees towards a holistic understanding of the world and their place within it. Her blessings are sought not only for academic success but also for spiritual enlightenment and the cultivation of virtues such as humility, compassion, and discernment.

The invocation of Saraswati is also significant in the context of Hindu rituals and religious ceremonies. Her presence is sought at the beginning of Vedic rituals, where hymns and mantras are recited to seek her blessings for clarity of mind and eloquence of speech. The Saraswati Vandana, a hymn dedicated to the goddess, is a common prayer recited by students and scholars before commencing their studies, asking for her guidance and inspiration. The mantra "Om Saraswati Namah" is often chanted to invoke her presence and seek her blessings for wisdom and knowledge.

Saraswati's influence transcends Hinduism and is recognized in other cultures and religions as well. In Buddhism, she is known as Benzaiten or Benten, the goddess of everything that flows, including water, words, speech, eloquence, music, and knowledge. She is venerated in Japan, where she is often depicted holding a biwa, a traditional Japanese lute. Benzaiten's worship reflects the cross-cultural reverence for the principles of wisdom and learning that Saraswati embodies. Similarly, in Jainism, Saraswati is revered as the goddess of knowledge and is invoked for her blessings in scholarly and intellectual pursuits.

The philosophical teachings associated with Saraswati also emphasize the importance of the pursuit of knowledge as a path to liberation (moksha). In Hinduism, the acquisition of knowledge is not merely for worldly success but is seen as a means to transcend ignorance and achieve spiritual liberation. The Upanishads, a collection of ancient Hindu texts, emphasize the pursuit of self-knowledge and the realization of the ultimate truth (Brahman) as the highest goal of human life. Saraswati, as the goddess of wisdom, guides her devotees on this path, helping them to overcome ignorance and attain self-realization.

Saraswati's significance is also evident in her various incarnations and manifestations, each representing different aspects of knowledge and wisdom. One of her well-known incarnations is as Savitri, the goddess of the Gayatri mantra. The Gayatri mantra, a highly revered Vedic hymn, is a prayer for spiritual illumination and wisdom. Savitri, as the personification of this mantra, embodies the highest aspirations of knowledge and spiritual enlightenment. Her invocation in the mantra highlights the central role of Saraswati in guiding the seeker towards the ultimate truth.

In South India, Saraswati is worshipped as Sharada, particularly in the temple town of Sringeri, which houses the Sharada Peetham, one of the four Advaita Vedanta monasteries established by the philosopher Adi Shankaracharya. The Sharada Peetham is a center of learning and scholarship, reflecting Saraswati's enduring presence in the intellectual and spiritual life of the region. Devotees seek her blessings for success in their academic and spiritual pursuits, emphasizing the goddess's role as a guiding light in the quest for knowledge.

Saraswati's relevance in contemporary times is particularly significant in the context of education and the pursuit of knowledge. In an era marked by rapid technological advancements and an abundance of information, the need for discernment and wisdom is more critical than ever. Saraswati's teachings remind us that true knowledge is not merely about the accumulation of information but involves the cultivation of wisdom, ethical conduct, and spiritual understanding. Her presence encourages a balanced approach to learning, one that integrates intellectual rigor with moral and spiritual growth.

The invocation of Saraswati also serves as a reminder of the transformative power of education. Education is seen as a means to empower individuals, uplift communities, and foster social and cultural development. Saraswati's blessings are sought by educators, students, and policymakers alike, who recognize the goddess's role in guiding the process of learning and enlightenment. Her teachings inspire a commitment to lifelong learning, intellectual curiosity, and the pursuit of excellence in all endeavors.

Saraswati, the goddess of wisdom and learning, embodies the ideals of intellectual and spiritual enlightenment. Her presence in Hindu mythology, religious practice, and cultural expressions underscores her enduring significance and universal appeal. As the patroness of the arts, sciences, and speech, she guides her devotees towards a holistic understanding of the world, fostering a deeper connection with the divine. Saraswati's teachings emphasize the importance of knowledge, creativity, and discernment, inspiring individuals to pursue a life of wisdom, compassion, and spiritual fulfillment. Through her blessings, Saraswati illuminates the path to self-realization, guiding us towards the ultimate goal of liberation and unity with the divine.

ᗡᗡᗡ

"Tulsi, the sacred plant, embodies purity and devotion. Her presence in homes and temples signifies the importance of nurturing the divine in everyday life. Through her, we learn the value of holistic health and ecological harmony."

FIVE

KALI: THE FIERCE PROTECTOR AND DESTROYER

Kali, the fierce protector and destroyer, stands as one of the most complex and potent deities in Hindu mythology. Her imagery is striking, often depicted with a dark complexion, disheveled hair, and a garland of skulls. She embodies the paradoxical nature of the divine feminine, combining aspects of destruction and protection, death and regeneration. Kali's role as a goddess transcends mere symbolism; she represents the raw, primal energy of the universe, the force that destroys illusion and ego, paving the way for spiritual liberation.

The origins of Kali are rooted in ancient Hindu texts, where she emerges as a powerful manifestation of the goddess Parvati, the consort of Shiva. According to one of the most famous myths, Kali was born from the forehead of Durga during a fierce battle against the demon Raktabija. Raktabija had the boon that every drop of his blood that touched the ground would create a new demon. As Durga struggled to defeat him, she became enraged and from her forehead sprang Kali, a ferocious form capable of consuming the demons. Kali drank Raktabija's blood before it could fall to the ground, thereby preventing more demons from spawning and securing victory for the gods. This tale highlights Kali's role as a fierce protector, who destroys evil to uphold cosmic order.

Kali's iconography is replete with symbolic elements that reflect her multifaceted nature. She is often depicted with four arms, holding a sword, a severed head, a bowl catching the blood, and a hand in the gesture of fearlessness (abhaya mudra). The sword represents divine knowledge, the severed head signifies the annihilation of the ego, the bowl catching blood symbolizes the destruction of ignorance, and the abhaya mudra offers reassurance to her devotees. Her tongue is often depicted sticking out, which according to some interpretations signifies her bloodthirsty nature, while others see it as a symbol of her insatiable thirst for justice and truth. Her nakedness represents her absolute freedom from illusion and pretense, emphasizing her connection to the primal and fundamental truths of existence.

Kali's dark and fearsome appearance can be intimidating, but it is essential to understand that her fearsome aspect is a reflection of her role as a destroyer of evil. She embodies the transformative power of time and death, which are necessary for the renewal and continuation of life. In Hindu philosophy, destruction is not viewed negatively but as an essential aspect of the cyclical nature of the universe, where creation, preservation, and destruction are interdependent processes. Kali's destructive force is thus an integral part of the cosmic balance, ensuring that old and obsolete forms are cleared away to make room for new growth and transformation.

One of the profound aspects of Kali's worship is the concept of facing and overcoming fear. Devotees of Kali are encouraged to confront their deepest fears and attachments, understanding that true liberation comes from transcending these limitations. Kali's fierce form is a reminder that spiritual growth often involves facing uncomfortable and challenging truths about oneself and the world. By embracing Kali's transformative energy, devotees can break free from the illusions and attachments that bind them, achieving a deeper sense of spiritual freedom and enlightenment.

Kali's association with time (Kala) further underscores her role as a destroyer. Time is an unstoppable force that consumes all things, and Kali, as its personification, represents the inevitable process of decay and destruction that precedes renewal. This aspect of Kali is particularly significant in the context of spiritual practice, where the awareness of time's passage can inspire a sense of urgency and dedication in one's quest for liberation. By recognizing the impermanence of all things, devotees are encouraged to focus on the pursuit of eternal truths and spiritual goals, rather than being distracted by the transient and fleeting aspects of material existence.

The worship of Kali is particularly prominent in Bengal, where she is revered as the mother goddess and protector of the region. The festival of Kali Puja, celebrated on the new moon night of the Hindu month of Kartik, is one of the most important religious events in Bengal. During this festival, devotees perform elaborate rituals, offer sacrifices, and recite hymns and mantras to invoke Kali's blessings. The festival emphasizes the themes of protection, destruction of evil, and spiritual renewal, with devotees seeking Kali's help in overcoming obstacles and achieving personal and spiritual goals.

In the tantric tradition, Kali holds a special place as a central deity. Tantra, which emphasizes the direct experience of the divine through rituals, meditation, and the harnessing of spiritual energies, views Kali as the embodiment of Shakti, the dynamic feminine principle of the universe. Tantric practices often involve the invocation of Kali's energy to awaken the kundalini, the dormant spiritual energy believed to reside at the base of the spine.

By awakening the kundalini and channeling it through the chakras, practitioners seek to achieve spiritual enlightenment and union with the divine. Kali, as the fierce and unrestrained aspect of Shakti, plays a crucial role in this transformative process, helping practitioners transcend their limitations and attain higher states of consciousness.

Kali's worship is not limited to India; she has also found a significant following in other cultures and religious traditions. In the West, Kali has been embraced by various spiritual movements and individuals seeking a deeper understanding of the divine feminine and the transformative power of destruction. Her image and symbolism have been adopted by modern spiritual seekers, artists, and writers, who find in her a powerful representation of female empowerment, liberation, and the embrace of the shadow aspects of the self. Kali's universal appeal lies in her ability to embody the complexities of existence, offering a path to transformation that involves confronting and integrating all aspects of the self, including those that are often feared or suppressed.

Kali's role as a protector is also reflected in her relationship with her devotees. She is often described as a fiercely compassionate mother who fiercely defends her children from harm. This maternal aspect of Kali is emphasized in the concept of "Kali Ma" (Mother Kali), where she is revered not just as a fearsome deity but as a nurturing and loving mother. Devotees seek her protection in times of trouble, believing that her powerful presence can dispel negative energies and provide strength and courage. The concept of divine motherhood is central to Kali's worship, highlighting the idea that true strength and protection come from a place of deep love and compassion.

The philosophical teachings associated with Kali also emphasize the importance of surrender and acceptance in the face of life's challenges. By surrendering to Kali's transformative power, devotees learn to let go of their attachments and fears, trusting in the divine process of destruction and renewal. This surrender is not a passive act but an active engagement with the deeper currents of existence, where one learns to flow with the changes and embrace the lessons that each experience brings. Kali's teachings encourage a radical acceptance of life in all its forms, recognizing that even the most difficult and painful experiences are opportunities for growth and transformation.

Kali's influence can be seen in various artistic and cultural expressions, from traditional temple art and sculptures to contemporary literature, music, and film. Her image is a powerful symbol of resistance, transformation, and the embrace of the shadow, resonating with those who seek to challenge the status quo and explore the depths of the human psyche. In literature, Kali has been depicted as both a fierce warrior and a compassionate mother, reflecting her complex and multifaceted nature. Her stories and myths continue to inspire new interpretations and adaptations, highlighting her enduring relevance and appeal.

In contemporary times, Kali's symbolism has been embraced by various social and political movements, particularly those advocating for women's rights and empowerment. Her fierce and unapologetic energy serves as an inspiration for individuals and groups seeking to challenge oppressive structures and reclaim their power. Kali's image as a warrior goddess resonates with those who are fighting for justice and equality, offering a powerful example of strength, resilience, and the transformative power of righteous anger.

Kali's teachings also have profound implications for personal and spiritual growth. By embracing Kali's energy, individuals can learn to confront their fears, integrate their shadow aspects, and achieve a deeper sense of self-awareness and empowerment. Her worship encourages a holistic approach to spirituality that acknowledges the importance of both light and darkness, creation and destruction, in the journey towards self-realization. Kali's presence serves as a reminder that true transformation involves embracing all aspects of existence, recognizing the divine in both the beautiful and the terrifying.

Kali, the fierce protector and destroyer, embodies the raw, primal energy of the universe and the transformative power of the divine feminine. Her role in Hindu mythology, religious practice, and cultural expressions underscores her significance as a powerful force for both destruction and protection, death and regeneration. Through her teachings, Kali encourages devotees to confront their fears, embrace their shadow aspects, and achieve spiritual liberation. Her influence extends beyond India, resonating with individuals and movements worldwide who seek to challenge oppressive structures, reclaim their power, and explore the depths of the human psyche. Kali's enduring relevance and universal appeal lie in her ability to embody the complexities of existence, offering a path to transformation that involves the radical acceptance and integration of all aspects of the self.

"Gayatri, the personification of the Vedic hymn, represents the pursuit of knowledge and enlightenment. Her teachings emphasize the transformative power of meditation and devotion. She guides us toward intellectual and spiritual growth."

SIX

PARVATI: THE GENTLE MOTHER AND NURTURER

Parvati, the gentle mother and nurturer, stands as a symbol of love, devotion, and compassion in Hindu mythology. She is revered as the consort of Lord Shiva, the destroyer in the Hindu trinity, and the mother of Ganesha and Kartikeya. Parvati embodies the ideal qualities of womanhood, combining strength and gentleness, devotion and independence, and compassion and wisdom. Her presence in Hindu culture and religion highlights the importance of the feminine divine as a nurturing and sustaining force in the universe.

The origins of Parvati are deeply rooted in Hindu mythology. She is believed to be an incarnation of Sati, the first wife of Shiva, who immolated herself in protest against her father's disrespect towards her husband. After Sati's death, Shiva withdrew into deep meditation, and the balance of the universe was threatened. The gods, seeking to restore harmony, invoked the goddess Adi Shakti, who incarnated as Parvati, the daughter of the mountain king Himavan and queen Mena. Parvati's name itself means "daughter of the mountains," reflecting her connection to nature and the earth.

Parvati's life story is one of devotion and perseverance. Despite being born into a royal family, she was drawn to the ascetic Shiva from an early age. Her love for Shiva was unwavering, and she undertook severe penances and austerities to win his heart. Her dedication and devotion ultimately moved Shiva, who accepted her as his consort. Their union symbolizes the perfect balance of masculine and feminine energies, the integration of asceticism and domesticity, and the harmonious coexistence of opposites.

Parvati's role as a mother is central to her identity. She is the mother of Ganesha, the elephant-headed god of wisdom and remover of obstacles, and Kartikeya, the god of war. As a mother, Parvati embodies nurturing, protection, and unconditional love. The stories of her interactions with her children highlight her patience, understanding, and gentle guidance. One of the most famous stories is that of Ganesha's creation. According to legend, Parvati created Ganesha from the sandalwood paste she used for her bath and breathed life into him. She appointed him as her guardian, instructing him not to let anyone enter while she bathed. When Shiva arrived and was denied entry by Ganesha, a battle ensued, resulting in Ganesha's head being severed. Parvati, heartbroken, implored Shiva to restore their son. Shiva replaced Ganesha's head with that of an elephant, granting him new life and making him one of the most beloved gods in the Hindu pantheon.

Parvati's nurturing nature extends beyond her immediate family. She is regarded as the mother of all living beings, a universal mother who provides love, care, and protection to all her children. This aspect of Parvati is especially emphasized in her role as Annapurna, the goddess of nourishment. Annapurna, meaning "giver of food," symbolizes Parvati's provision of sustenance and nourishment to the world. She is often depicted holding a ladle and a bowl of food, signifying her role in ensuring that no one goes hungry. Devotees seek her blessings for abundance and prosperity, and her worship emphasizes the importance of sharing and caring for others.

Parvati's gentle and nurturing qualities are complemented by her strength and independence. She is not just a devoted wife and mother but also a powerful goddess in her own right. In the form of Durga, Parvati takes on a warrior aspect, embodying strength and protection. Durga's role as a fierce protector of the righteous and destroyer of evil highlights Parvati's multifaceted nature. She is both gentle and formidable, capable of immense compassion and unwavering resolve. This duality reflects the complexity and depth of the feminine divine, challenging the simplistic notions of femininity as passive or weak.

Parvati's influence extends to various aspects of life and culture. She is worshipped as a symbol of marital bliss and domestic harmony. Married women seek her blessings for a happy and prosperous married life, while unmarried women pray to her for a suitable partner. The festival of Teej, celebrated in northern India, is dedicated to Parvati and Shiva's union. During this festival, women observe fasts and perform rituals to honor Parvati, seeking her blessings for marital happiness and longevity. The celebration of Teej highlights the cultural importance of Parvati as a model of devotion, love, and marital harmony.

Parvati is also associated with various forms of art and creativity. As the goddess of love and beauty, she inspires artistic expression in its many forms. Her influence can be seen in classical Indian dance, music, and literature, where themes of love, devotion, and feminine grace are prominently featured. Parvati's story and qualities are celebrated in numerous works of art, from intricate temple sculptures to devotional songs and poems. Her presence in the cultural imagination reflects her enduring significance and the deep connection between the divine feminine and creative expression.

The philosophical teachings associated with Parvati emphasize the importance of balance and integration. Her union with Shiva represents the harmonious blending of opposites: asceticism and domesticity, masculine and feminine, destruction and creation. This balance is not just a metaphysical concept but a practical guide for living a balanced and harmonious life. Parvati's teachings encourage individuals to embrace both their gentle and strong aspects, to find harmony in their relationships, and to seek a balanced approach to life's challenges.

Parvati's role as a nurturer and protector also extends to the natural world. As the daughter of the mountains, she is closely connected to nature and the environment. In many stories, she is depicted as living in harmony with the natural world, surrounded by animals and plants. This connection to nature underscores the importance of environmental stewardship and the need to protect and preserve the earth. Parvati's example encourages a respectful and nurturing relationship with the natural world, emphasizing the interconnectedness of all life.

In contemporary times, Parvati's symbolism and teachings continue to inspire and resonate with people around the world. Her qualities of love, devotion, and nurturing are universal values that transcend cultural and religious boundaries. Parvati's story serves as a reminder of the importance of compassion, perseverance, and balance in our lives. Her influence can be seen in various social and cultural movements that seek to empower women, promote environmental sustainability, and foster a sense of community and caring.

Parvati's worship also highlights the importance of the feminine divine in Hinduism. While the male gods often receive more attention, the goddesses play a crucial role in the spiritual and cultural life of Hinduism. Parvati, along with other goddesses like

Lakshmi, Saraswati, and Kali, embodies the diverse and dynamic nature of the divine feminine. Their worship reflects the recognition of the essential role that feminine energy plays in the universe, encompassing creation, sustenance, and transformation.

The stories and myths associated with Parvati provide rich insights into the values and beliefs of Hindu culture. They emphasize the importance of devotion, love, and service to others. Parvati's interactions with her family and the gods highlight the significance of relationships and the need for harmony and balance in all aspects of life. Her example encourages individuals to cultivate virtues such as patience, compassion, and resilience, and to find strength in their devotion and faith.

Parvati's teachings also have profound implications for personal and spiritual growth. Her journey of devotion and perseverance in winning Shiva's love serves as a powerful metaphor for the spiritual quest. It highlights the importance of dedication, discipline, and inner strength in achieving spiritual goals. Parvati's role as a mother and nurturer underscores the importance of caring for others and finding fulfillment in service and love. Her example encourages individuals to seek a higher purpose and to find meaning and joy in their relationships and contributions to the world.

Parvati, the gentle mother and nurturer, embodies the ideals of love, devotion, and compassion in Hindu mythology. Her presence in Hindu culture and religion highlights the importance of the feminine divine as a nurturing and sustaining force in the universe. Parvati's life story and qualities provide valuable lessons on the importance of balance, perseverance, and compassion. Her worship reflects the recognition of the essential role that feminine energy plays in the cosmos, encompassing creation, sustenance, and transformation. Through her teachings and example, Parvati inspires individuals to cultivate virtues such as love, devotion, and resilience, and to seek harmony and balance in their lives. Her enduring significance and universal appeal lie in her ability to embody the diverse and dynamic nature of the divine feminine, offering a path to personal and spiritual growth that encompasses both strength and gentleness, devotion and independence.

"Bhumi, the Earth Goddess, is the nurturing and sustaining force of the planet. Her worship emphasizes our deep connection to the Earth and the need for ecological stewardship. She reminds us of the interconnectedness of all life."

SEVEN
SITA: THE EMBODIMENT OF VIRTUE AND DEVOTION

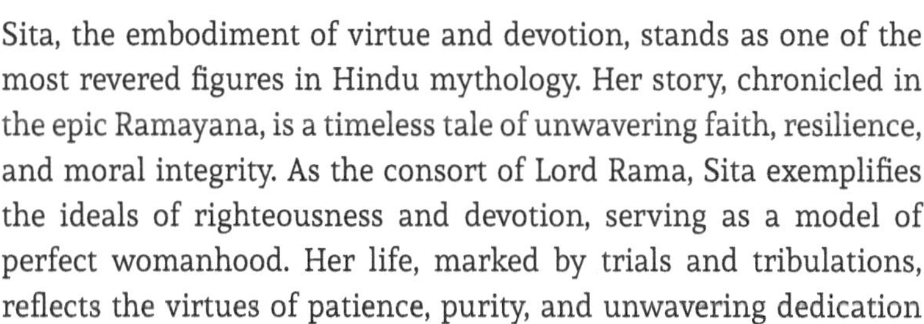

Sita, the embodiment of virtue and devotion, stands as one of the most revered figures in Hindu mythology. Her story, chronicled in the epic Ramayana, is a timeless tale of unwavering faith, resilience, and moral integrity. As the consort of Lord Rama, Sita exemplifies the ideals of righteousness and devotion, serving as a model of perfect womanhood. Her life, marked by trials and tribulations, reflects the virtues of patience, purity, and unwavering dedication to dharma, the cosmic law that upholds the universe.

Sita's origins are shrouded in divine mystery. According to the Ramayana, she was discovered as an infant in a furrow by King Janaka while he was plowing the field as part of a ritual to invoke rains. Recognizing her as a divine gift, King Janaka adopted her as his daughter. Sita's birth from the earth aligns her with Bhumi Devi, the goddess of the earth, symbolizing her intrinsic connection to nature and purity. Raised in the royal household of Mithila, Sita grew up imbued with virtues and wisdom, reflecting her divine heritage.

Sita's marriage to Rama is one of the central events of the Ramayana, symbolizing the union of dharma and devotion. The story of her Swayamvara, a ceremony where she chose her husband, is a testament to her strength and virtue. King Janaka declared that Sita would marry the prince who could string the mighty bow of Shiva. Many princes tried and failed, but Rama, the prince of Ayodhya, succeeded effortlessly, thus winning Sita's hand in marriage. This event highlights the divine destiny that binds Sita and Rama, a union ordained by cosmic forces.

Sita's life with Rama in Ayodhya was marked by mutual love, respect, and devotion. She supported Rama through his duties as a prince and shared in his joys and challenges. However, their happiness was short-lived, as Rama was exiled to the forest for fourteen years due to palace intrigues. Sita, embodying the principles of loyalty and devotion, insisted on accompanying Rama into exile, despite the hardships it entailed. Her decision to leave behind the comforts of the palace and embrace the rigors of forest life underscores her unwavering commitment to her husband and her adherence to dharma.

The period of exile in the forest was a time of great trial for Sita, but also one where her virtues shone brightly. She adapted to the austere life in the forest with grace and resilience, finding joy in the simple pleasures of nature. Her devotion to Rama remained steadfast, and her presence provided him with strength and solace. Sita's experiences during the exile also highlighted her compassion and kindness, as she befriended and aided the forest dwellers, embodying the ideal of selfless service.

One of the most defining episodes in Sita's life is her abduction by Ravana, the demon king of Lanka. Ravana, enamored by Sita's beauty, kidnapped her while Rama and his brother Lakshmana were away. Sita's ordeal in Lanka is a testament to her unyielding virtue and strength of character. Despite being imprisoned and subjected to Ravana's advances, she remained steadfast in her devotion to Rama, rejecting Ravana's propositions with unwavering resolve. Her purity and faith became her shield, protecting her from Ravana's advances and preserving her honor.

Sita's period of captivity in Lanka also highlights her profound inner strength and spiritual fortitude. Isolated and surrounded by enemies, she found solace in her unwavering faith in Rama and her adherence to dharma. Her prayers and meditations sustained her, providing her with the strength to endure her trials. Sita's rejection of Ravana's temptations and her steadfast adherence to her principles illustrate her moral integrity and spiritual resilience, making her a beacon of virtue and devotion.

The rescue of Sita by Rama, with the help of Hanuman and the monkey army, is a pivotal moment in the Ramayana. This event is not just a physical rescue but a triumph of dharma over adharma, good over evil. Sita's reunion with Rama is marked by joy and relief, but also by a painful test of her chastity. To dispel any doubts about her purity, Sita willingly underwent the trial by fire, known as Agni Pariksha. Emerging unscathed from the flames, she demonstrated her purity and fidelity, reinforcing her status as an embodiment of virtue and devotion.

Sita's return to Ayodhya marked the end of their exile and the beginning of Rama's reign as king. However, her trials were not over. Despite her proven chastity, rumors about her purity persisted among the people of Ayodhya. To uphold his duty as a king and to quell public dissent, Rama made the heart-wrenching decision to send Sita into exile once again, this time to the hermitage of sage Valmiki. Sita, pregnant and alone, accepted her fate with grace and dignity, demonstrating her unshakable faith in dharma and her willingness to sacrifice her own happiness for the greater good.

During her time at Valmiki's hermitage, Sita gave birth to her twin sons, Lava and Kusha. She raised them with love and care, instilling in them the values of righteousness and devotion. Sita's role as a mother is a testament to her nurturing spirit and her ability to impart wisdom and virtue to her children. The reunion of Rama with Lava and Kusha, orchestrated by Valmiki, brought Sita's story full circle, highlighting the enduring bond between her and Rama.

The final act of Sita's life is both poignant and profound. When Rama sought to bring her back to Ayodhya, Sita, weary of the trials and accusations, invoked her mother, the earth, to take her back. The earth opened up and Sita returned to her divine abode, symbolizing her return to purity and divinity. This act of returning to the earth signifies Sita's transcendence of worldly trials and her ultimate union with the divine. It underscores her status as an embodiment of virtue and devotion, whose life and actions were governed by unwavering adherence to dharma.

Sita's story, as told in the Ramayana, has profound philosophical and spiritual implications. She embodies the ideal of dharma, illustrating how adherence to righteousness and moral integrity can guide one through the most challenging circumstances. Sita's unwavering faith and devotion serve as a model for all devotees, showing that true strength lies in inner purity and steadfastness to one's principles. Her life teaches the importance of patience, resilience, and the transformative power of love and devotion.

The cultural and religious significance of Sita extends beyond the Ramayana. She is venerated as a goddess and an ideal woman in Hindu tradition. Temples dedicated to Sita, such as the Janaki Mandir in Nepal, attract devotees who seek her blessings for strength, virtue, and marital harmony. Festivals celebrating her life, such as Sita Navami, highlight her enduring legacy and the values she represents. Through prayers, rituals, and stories, Sita's virtues are passed down through generations, reinforcing her role as a symbol of devotion and righteousness.

Sita's influence also extends to various cultural expressions, including literature, art, and theater. Her story has inspired countless adaptations and interpretations, each highlighting different aspects of her character and virtues. In classical Indian dance forms such as Bharatanatyam and Kathak, performances of the Ramayana often emphasize Sita's grace, strength, and devotion. Her image is a common motif in Indian art, depicted in paintings, sculptures, and textiles, reflecting her central place in the cultural imagination.

In contemporary times, Sita's story continues to resonate with people around the world. Her virtues of devotion, resilience, and moral integrity are universal values that transcend cultural and religious boundaries. Sita's example inspires individuals to face their challenges with courage and faith, to uphold their principles in the face of adversity, and to find strength in their devotion and love. Her story serves as a reminder of the power of inner strength and the enduring importance of righteousness and virtue.

Sita's life also offers valuable lessons for gender dynamics and the role of women in society. She embodies the ideals of strength and independence, challenging the notion of passive femininity. Sita's unwavering adherence to her principles, even in the face of immense challenges, highlights the importance of women's autonomy and moral agency. Her story encourages a reexamination of traditional gender roles, advocating for a more inclusive and empowering understanding of womanhood.

Moreover, Sita's narrative underscores the significance of love and devotion in personal and spiritual growth. Her relationship with Rama, marked by mutual respect and devotion, serves as a model for ideal partnerships. Sita's life teaches that true devotion involves both love and sacrifice, and that the highest form of love is selfless and unconditional. Her story inspires individuals to cultivate deep and meaningful relationships, grounded in mutual respect, support, and devotion.

Sita, the embodiment of virtue and devotion, stands as a timeless symbol of righteousness, love, and resilience. Her story, chronicled in the Ramayana, provides profound insights into the ideals of dharma and the transformative power of devotion. Sita's unwavering faith, moral integrity, and compassionate nature make her an enduring figure of inspiration and reverence. Her legacy, celebrated through religious rituals, cultural expressions, and personal devotion, continues to inspire individuals to uphold the values of virtue, devotion, and righteousness in their own lives. Through her teachings and example, Sita offers a path to personal and spiritual growth, guiding individuals towards a life of inner strength, moral integrity, and unwavering devotion.

"Manasa, the serpent goddess of fertility and health, embodies the protective and healing aspects of the divine feminine. Her story highlights the importance of respecting and protecting the natural world. Through her, we understand the cycles of life and renewal."

EIGHT

RADHA: THE SYMBOL OF DIVINE LOVE

Radha, the symbol of divine love, holds a unique and revered place in Hindu mythology. Her love for Krishna transcends the mortal realm and embodies the highest form of spiritual devotion and union. Radha's story, primarily recounted in the Bhagavata Purana, the Gita Govinda, and various other texts and folklore, is a timeless tale of love, longing, and spiritual fulfillment. Her relationship with Krishna represents the soul's intense yearning for union with the divine, making Radha a profound symbol of pure, selfless love and devotion.

Radha's origins are enveloped in mystery and divine enchantment. She is often depicted as a cowherd girl from the village of Vrindavan, where Krishna spent his childhood. Radha is considered to be the daughter of Vrishabhanu and Kirti, though some traditions describe her as an incarnation of Lakshmi, the goddess of fortune, born to be united with Krishna. Her birth, much like Krishna's, is believed to be divinely ordained, destined to play a pivotal role in the spiritual narrative of divine love and devotion.

The bond between Radha and Krishna is one of the most celebrated aspects of Hindu mythology. Their relationship is not merely a romantic one but symbolizes the eternal and transcendental love between the individual soul (jivatma) and the supreme soul (paramatma). Radha's love for Krishna is depicted as intense and unwavering, reflecting the highest form of bhakti (devotion) known as madhurya bhava, or the mood of sweetness. This form of devotion transcends physical and emotional boundaries, reaching a spiritual pinnacle where the lover and the beloved become one.

The stories of Radha and Krishna's love are filled with enchanting episodes of their divine play (lila) in the forests of Vrindavan. These tales are rich in symbolism and spiritual significance, illustrating the dynamics of divine love and the soul's journey towards spiritual enlightenment. The Ras Lila, or the dance of divine love, is one of the most famous episodes, where Krishna dances with Radha and the gopis (cowherd girls) in the moonlit groves of Vrindavan. During this divine dance, Krishna multiplies himself to be with each gopi, symbolizing the omnipresence of the divine and the intimate relationship each soul can have with God. Radha, however, remains the central figure, the epitome of devotion and the embodiment of the supreme love that transcends all.

Radha's love for Krishna is marked by intense longing and separation, known as viraha. This aspect of their relationship highlights the pain and ecstasy of divine love, where the absence of the beloved intensifies the yearning and deepens the spiritual connection. The theme of separation is profoundly explored in the Gita Govinda, a lyrical poem by the 12th-century poet Jayadeva, which depicts Radha's sorrow and longing for Krishna when he is away. Her love is portrayed as selfless and all-consuming, where the joy of union and the pain of separation are seen as two sides of the same coin, both leading to a deeper spiritual awakening and union with the divine.

Radha's devotion to Krishna is not confined to their youthful pastimes but extends to a profound spiritual bond that transcends time and space. She is often depicted as the supreme devotee, whose love and devotion for Krishna are unparalleled. This makes Radha an important figure in the Bhakti movement, where devotees seek to emulate her pure and selfless love for God. The Bhakti tradition, which emphasizes personal devotion and the direct relationship between the devotee and the divine, finds its highest expression in Radha's love for Krishna. Her devotion is seen as the ultimate path to spiritual liberation, where love becomes the means and the end of the spiritual journey.

The symbolism of Radha's love also extends to the concept of divine feminine energy (Shakti) and its relationship with the divine masculine (Shiva). In many traditions, Radha is seen as the embodiment of Shakti, the dynamic energy that activates and complements the divine consciousness represented by Krishna. This union of Shakti and Shiva, or Radha and Krishna, symbolizes the perfect harmony and balance of cosmic energies, the dynamic interplay that sustains the universe. Radha's role as the divine consort underscores the importance of feminine energy in the spiritual and cosmic order, highlighting the integral and complementary nature of the masculine and feminine principles.

Radha's influence is not limited to religious texts and rituals but permeates various forms of art, literature, and culture. Her story has inspired countless works of poetry, music, dance, and painting, each celebrating the beauty and profundity of divine love. Classical Indian dance forms like Bharatanatyam and Kathak often depict episodes from Radha and Krishna's life, using expressive gestures and movements to convey the emotions of love, longing, and devotion. The Radha-Krishna theme is a common motif in Indian miniature paintings, where artists have depicted their divine love in vibrant and intricate compositions.

In poetry, Radha's love for Krishna has been a source of inspiration for many poets and saints. The Ashtapadis of Jayadeva's Gita

Govinda, the poems of Vidyapati, and the songs of the North Indian saint-poet Mirabai are some of the literary works that extol Radha's devotion and the bliss of divine love. These works explore the emotional depth and spiritual ecstasy of Radha's love, portraying it as the ultimate form of devotion that leads to the realization of the divine.

Radha's symbolism also resonates in contemporary spiritual and cultural contexts. Her story of unconditional love and devotion continues to inspire people across different cultures and traditions. The celebration of Radha's love for Krishna in festivals like Janmashtami (Krishna's birthday) and Radhashtami (Radha's birthday) brings together communities in joyous devotion and celebration. These festivals highlight the timeless appeal of Radha's story and its ability to evoke deep spiritual emotions and connections among devotees.

Radha's narrative also offers valuable insights into the nature of divine love and its transformative power. Her love for Krishna is not possessive or conditional but pure and selfless, reflecting the highest ideals of spiritual love. This form of love transcends the ego and personal desires, leading to a state of oneness with the beloved. Radha's example teaches that true love involves surrender and devotion, where the lover's identity merges with the beloved, and all distinctions dissolve in the unity of divine love.

Moreover, Radha's story underscores the importance of the feminine principle in spiritual practice. Her role as the supreme devotee and the embodiment of divine love highlights the power and significance of feminine energy in the spiritual path. Radha's love for Krishna represents the active and dynamic aspect of devotion, where love becomes a powerful force that drives the soul towards spiritual realization. This recognition of the feminine divine challenges patriarchal notions and emphasizes the integral role of feminine qualities like love, compassion, and intuition in spiritual growth.

Radha's influence extends beyond Hinduism, resonating with spiritual seekers and mystics from various traditions. Her story of divine love finds parallels in other mystical traditions, where the soul's longing for union with the divine is a common theme. In Sufism, for example, the relationship between the lover (the devotee) and the beloved (God) is central to the spiritual path, mirroring the dynamics of Radha and Krishna's love. The poetry of Rumi and other Sufi mystics often echoes the sentiments of longing and divine union found in Radha's devotion to Krishna.

In contemporary times, Radha's story continues to inspire and guide individuals on their spiritual journeys. Her example of pure and selfless love offers a powerful antidote to the materialism and ego-driven pursuits of modern life. By focusing on the higher ideals of love and devotion, Radha's teachings encourage individuals to seek deeper connections and spiritual fulfillment. Her story serves as a reminder that true happiness and liberation lie in the selfless love and devotion to the divine.

Radha, as the symbol of divine love, embodies the highest ideals of devotion, purity, and spiritual fulfillment. Her relationship with Krishna transcends the physical and emotional realms, reaching the pinnacle of spiritual union. Radha's story, rich in symbolism and spiritual significance, offers profound insights into the nature of divine love and its transformative power. Her unwavering devotion and selfless love for Krishna serve as a model for all spiritual seekers, guiding them towards the ultimate goal of union with the divine. Through her teachings and example, Radha continues to inspire and uplift, reminding us of the timeless and universal nature of divine love.

ॐॐॐ

"Santoshi Mata, the Mother of Satisfaction, teaches the values of patience, perseverance, and devotion. Her worship brings peace and contentment to our lives. She is a beacon of hope and harmony in familial and personal life."

NINE

GANGA: THE PURIFIER AND LIFE-GIVING RIVER GODDESS

Ganga, the purifier and life-giving river goddess, holds an unparalleled place in Hindu mythology and Indian culture. She is not merely a river but a divine entity, revered for her purifying and life-sustaining qualities. Her story, interwoven with legends and religious practices, symbolizes purity, forgiveness, and the continuous flow of life. Ganga's presence is deeply embedded in the spiritual and cultural fabric of India, embodying the essence of both physical sustenance and spiritual salvation.

According to Hindu mythology, Ganga originated from the heavens. She is considered the daughter of the mountain king Himavan and queen Mena, making her the sister of Parvati, Shiva's consort. Ganga's descent from the heavens to the earth is a central theme in her story. The legend of her descent, known as the Ganga Avatarnana, tells of King Bhagiratha's intense penance to bring Ganga to the earth to purify the ashes of his ancestors and grant them salvation. Impressed by his devotion, the gods granted his wish, but there was a significant challenge: Ganga's powerful descent could devastate the earth. To mitigate this, Lord Shiva caught Ganga in his matted locks, releasing her gently in streams to flow across the earth. This act of Shiva not only saved the earth from destruction but also sanctified Ganga, making her a bridge between the heavens and the earth.

The Ganga's sacredness is reinforced by her association with Shiva, who is often depicted with the river flowing from his hair. This imagery symbolizes the union of cosmic energy and divine grace. Ganga's descent is not just a physical event but a spiritual one, representing the flow of divine grace into the world, purifying and uplifting human souls. Her waters are believed to cleanse sins, heal the sick, and bring liberation to those who bathe in them with faith.

Ganga's role as a purifier is central to her identity. In Hindu rituals, the waters of the Ganga, known as Gangajal, are considered essential for purifying and sanctifying ceremonies. Gangajal is used in various rites, from birth to death, symbolizing the river's life-giving and purifying properties. The belief in Ganga's purifying power is so strong that even a few drops of her water are thought to purify anything they touch. This faith in her cleansing ability underscores the deep spiritual connection between the river and her devotees.

The city of Varanasi, one of the oldest continuously inhabited cities in the world, holds a special place in the worship of Ganga. Situated on the banks of the river, Varanasi is considered the spiritual capital of India. Pilgrims from all over the country and beyond come to Varanasi to bathe in the Ganga's sacred waters and perform rituals for their ancestors. The ghats (steps leading to the river) of Varanasi are alive with activity from dawn to dusk, as people engage in prayers, offerings, and ceremonies. The Ganga Aarti, a daily ritual performed on the ghats, is a spectacular sight, with priests chanting hymns and waving oil lamps in elaborate patterns, creating a mesmerizing atmosphere that reflects the deep reverence for the river goddess.

Ganga's life-giving properties extend beyond her spiritual significance. The river is a vital source of water for millions of people, supporting agriculture, providing drinking water, and sustaining ecosystems. The Ganges Basin, covering a vast area of northern India and Bangladesh, is one of the most fertile and densely populated regions in the world. The river's waters irrigate fields that produce a significant portion of India's food supply, making Ganga indispensable to the country's food security and economy. The life-giving aspect of Ganga is celebrated in various festivals and rituals that honor her as the nurturer and sustainer of life.

However, Ganga's role as a life-giver is not without challenges. The river faces significant pollution from industrial waste, sewage, and plastic, threatening its health and the well-being of those who depend on it. This environmental degradation has sparked numerous efforts to clean and protect the river. The Indian government has launched initiatives like the Namami Gange program, aimed at rejuvenating the Ganga by addressing pollution and improving water quality. These efforts reflect the recognition of Ganga's critical importance and the need to preserve her sanctity for future generations.

The mythology surrounding Ganga also highlights her compassionate nature. She is often depicted as a benevolent mother, willing to undergo hardships for the sake of her devotees. One poignant story tells of her descent to the netherworlds to rescue the souls trapped there. This tale illustrates Ganga's willingness to go to great lengths to bring salvation to those in need, reinforcing her role as a merciful and loving goddess. Her compassion is a central theme in her worship, with devotees seeking her blessings for forgiveness, healing, and protection.

The Ganga's journey from the Himalayas to the Bay of Bengal is symbolic of the spiritual journey from the material world to liberation. As the river flows through different terrains, it mirrors the human soul's journey through the trials and tribulations of life, moving towards spiritual enlightenment and liberation. This symbolism is reflected in the numerous pilgrimage sites along the river's course, each with its own spiritual significance. Pilgrims travel from the source of the Ganga in the Gangotri Glacier to her confluence with the ocean in the Ganges Delta, undertaking a journey that is both physical and spiritual.

The artistic and cultural expressions inspired by Ganga further illustrate her profound impact on Indian life. The river has been the muse for countless poets, writers, and artists. In classical Indian literature, Ganga is often personified as a beautiful and nurturing goddess, her story woven into epic tales and devotional songs. Paintings and sculptures of Ganga adorn temples and public spaces, depicting her serene and majestic presence. Folk traditions and festivals along the river celebrate her, with songs and dances expressing the deep emotional and spiritual connection people have with her.

In addition to her cultural and spiritual significance, Ganga represents the eternal flow of time and the cyclical nature of life and death. Her waters are seen as a link between the past, present, and future, carrying the memories and aspirations of generations. The practice of immersing ashes of the deceased in the Ganga reflects the belief that the river provides a pathway to moksha (liberation), dissolving the bonds of karma and facilitating the soul's journey to the divine. This practice underscores the river's role as a bridge between the mortal and the eternal, offering solace and hope to the living.

Ganga's influence extends beyond Hinduism, touching other religious and cultural traditions in India. In Buddhism, she is revered as a sacred river, and her waters are used in various rituals and ceremonies. The river also holds significance in Jainism, where she is venerated for her purity and life-giving properties. This cross-religious reverence highlights Ganga's universal appeal as a symbol of purity, sustenance, and spiritual grace.

In contemporary times, the Ganga continues to be a source of inspiration and a focal point for environmental and social movements. Activists and spiritual leaders emphasize the need to protect and restore the river, advocating for sustainable practices and raising awareness about the ecological and cultural importance of Ganga. The river's plight has become a rallying point for broader discussions on environmental justice, water management, and the interconnectedness of natural and human systems. Efforts to clean and rejuvenate the Ganga are seen as part of a larger commitment to preserving the planet's natural heritage and ensuring a sustainable future for all.

Ganga's enduring legacy as the purifier and life-giving river goddess is a testament to her profound impact on Indian spirituality, culture, and ecology. Her story, rich with symbolism and divine grace, offers valuable lessons on the importance of purity, compassion, and the continuous flow of life. The river's sacredness and life-sustaining properties underscore the interconnectedness of the physical and spiritual realms, reflecting the belief that water is not just a resource but a divine gift that sustains and purifies life. Through her teachings and presence, Ganga inspires a deep reverence for nature and a commitment to preserving the sacred and life-giving qualities of the natural world.

ﭬﭬﭬ

"Kamakhya, the goddess of desire and fertility, celebrates the sacredness of the feminine body. Her worship embraces the transformative power of desire as a path to spiritual enlightenment. She embodies the primal forces of nature and fertility."

TEN

ANNAPURNA: THE GODDESS OF NOURISHMENT

Annapurna, the goddess of nourishment, embodies the essential sustenance that supports all life. Her name, derived from the Sanskrit words "Anna" meaning food and "Purna" meaning complete or full, signifies her role as the provider of food and nourishment. In Hindu tradition, Annapurna is revered as a benevolent and generous deity, ensuring that her devotees are well-fed and their needs are met. Her story and symbolism reflect the fundamental importance of food in human life, not just as a physical necessity but as a sacred offering that sustains and nurtures the body and soul.

Annapurna's origins are closely linked to her association with Lord Shiva, one of the principal deities in Hinduism. According to legend, there was once a time when the world was plagued by famine, and food became scarce. The people, suffering from hunger and deprivation, prayed to Shiva for relief. Moved by their plight, Shiva sought the help of Parvati, his consort. Parvati, embodying compassion and maternal care, transformed into Annapurna, the goddess of nourishment. She appeared in the city of Kashi (Varanasi), distributing food to all who came to her. Shiva, recognizing her divine role, approached Annapurna with an empty begging bowl, symbolizing his recognition of the importance of food and the goddess's power to provide it. Annapurna filled Shiva's bowl, thus emphasizing the interconnectedness of the divine and the material world, and the sanctity of nourishment.

The imagery of Annapurna is rich with symbolic elements that underscore her role as the provider of sustenance. She is often depicted as a beautiful woman adorned with ornaments and a serene expression, holding a ladle in one hand and a bowl of food in the other. The ladle represents her role in distributing nourishment, while the bowl signifies abundance and the fulfillment of hunger. Sometimes she is shown seated on a throne, surrounded by lush vegetation and bountiful harvests, highlighting her connection to the earth's fertility and the cycles of nature. This portrayal emphasizes that food is not just a material necessity but a divine blessing, a gift from the goddess that sustains life.

Annapurna's significance extends beyond the mythological and symbolic realms into the practical aspects of daily life and religious practice. In Hindu households, the kitchen is often regarded as a sacred space, and cooking is seen as an act of devotion. Food prepared in the kitchen is offered to the deities before being consumed, symbolizing gratitude for the nourishment provided by the divine. Annapurna, as the goddess of nourishment, is invoked to bless the food and ensure that it is pure and sustaining. This practice reflects the deep cultural and spiritual significance of food in Hinduism, where it is not merely fuel for the body but a sacred offering that nurtures the soul.

The festival of Annakut, celebrated primarily in Gujarat and Maharashtra, is dedicated to Annapurna and the abundance of food she provides. During Annakut, a grand feast is prepared with a variety of dishes, which are then offered to the deities in a ceremonial display. This feast, symbolizing the mountain of food, is shared among the community, emphasizing the values of sharing, gratitude, and the joy of communal eating. The festival underscores the belief that food is a divine gift to be cherished and shared, reinforcing Annapurna's role as the nurturer and sustainer of life.

Annapurna's teachings also highlight the importance of food security and the ethical responsibility to ensure that no one goes hungry. In a world where hunger and malnutrition remain significant challenges, her symbolism serves as a reminder of the moral duty to care for the less fortunate and to strive for a just and equitable distribution of resources. This ethical dimension is reflected in various social and charitable practices inspired by Annapurna's ideals. Food distribution programs, community kitchens, and initiatives to combat hunger and food wastage are often undertaken in her name, embodying her compassionate and nurturing spirit.

The concept of Annapurna also extends to the broader understanding of nourishment, encompassing not only physical food but also spiritual and emotional sustenance. Just as the body needs food to survive, the mind and soul require nourishment to thrive. Annapurna's blessings are sought not only for physical well-being but also for inner peace, wisdom, and spiritual growth. This holistic view of nourishment reflects the interconnectedness of the physical and spiritual aspects of life, where true sustenance involves nurturing all dimensions of being.

In many temples dedicated to Annapurna, particularly the famous Annapurna Devi Mandir in Varanasi, food is distributed to devotees and the needy as a form of prasad (divine offering). This practice reinforces the idea that feeding others is a sacred act, a form of worship that honors the goddess and her role as the provider of nourishment. The temple's kitchen, known as the Annapurna kitchen, operates continuously, ensuring that no one who seeks the goddess's blessings goes hungry. This tradition of serving food to all, regardless of social or economic status, highlights the inclusive and compassionate nature of Annapurna's worship.

Annapurna's influence is also evident in the cultural and artistic expressions of Hinduism. Songs, hymns, and devotional poetry dedicated to her celebrate her generosity and the sanctity of food. These artistic forms often depict the goddess in her benevolent aspect, showering blessings and providing sustenance to her devotees. The portrayal of Annapurna in art and literature serves as a reminder of the essential role of nourishment in human life and the divine grace that makes it possible.

In contemporary times, the values associated with Annapurna's worship are particularly relevant in addressing global challenges related to food security, sustainability, and environmental stewardship. The goddess's association with the earth's fertility and the cycles of nature underscores the importance of sustainable agricultural practices and the need to protect natural resources. By honoring Annapurna, individuals and communities are encouraged to adopt practices that promote the health and well-being of the planet, ensuring that the earth continues to provide for future generations.

Annapurna's teachings also emphasize the importance of gratitude and mindfulness in the act of eating. In a fast-paced world where meals are often consumed hurriedly and without reflection, her example encourages a more mindful approach to food. Taking time to appreciate the food, recognizing the efforts of those who produce and prepare it, and offering gratitude to the divine for the nourishment it provides are practices that deepen the connection between food and spirituality. This mindful approach to eating fosters a greater appreciation for the sustenance we receive and encourages a more respectful and conscious relationship with food.

The philosophy of Annapurna also intersects with the principles of Ayurveda, the ancient Indian system of medicine that emphasizes the balance of body, mind, and spirit. In Ayurveda, food is considered a vital component of health and well-being, with the understanding that what we eat directly affects our physical and mental states. Annapurna's role as the goddess of nourishment aligns with the Ayurvedic principles of mindful eating, balanced nutrition, and the healing properties of food. By invoking Annapurna's blessings, practitioners of Ayurveda seek to harmonize their diets with the rhythms of nature, promoting overall health and vitality.

Annapurna's enduring legacy as the goddess of nourishment is a testament to her profound impact on Hindu spirituality, culture, and daily life. Her story and symbolism highlight the essential role of food in sustaining life and the deep spiritual significance of nourishment. Through her teachings, Annapurna inspires a holistic understanding of sustenance that encompasses physical, emotional, and spiritual well-being. Her worship encourages practices of gratitude, mindfulness, and ethical responsibility, fostering a compassionate and inclusive approach to food and nourishment. By honoring Annapurna, individuals and communities are reminded of the sacredness of food and the divine grace that sustains all life, guiding them towards a more balanced, mindful, and harmonious existence.

ᢒᢒᢒ

"Chandi, the fierce form of Shakti, is a powerful protector and warrior. Her story is a testament to the importance of confronting and overcoming adversity. She inspires us to embrace our inner strength and resilience."

ELEVEN

MEENAKSHI: THE QUEEN OF MADURAI

Meenakshi, the Queen of Madurai, is one of the most celebrated and revered goddesses in the Hindu pantheon. Her story, deeply intertwined with the history and culture of Madurai, a city in Tamil Nadu, India, embodies the ideals of beauty, strength, and divine authority. Meenakshi is a manifestation of Parvati, the consort of Shiva, and is unique among goddesses for her role as a warrior queen and sovereign. The legend of Meenakshi highlights the fusion of divine and royal power, making her a central figure in the religious and cultural life of Madurai.

The origin of Meenakshi is rooted in ancient mythology and legend. According to tradition, she was born to the Pandya king Malayadwaja and his queen Kanchanamalai, who were childless and yearned for a successor. They performed intense penance and sacrifices to the gods, praying for a child. Their prayers were answered when Meenakshi emerged from the sacrificial fire as a three-year-old girl with three breasts, an unusual but divine sign. A celestial voice informed the king and queen that the third breast would disappear when she met her destined husband.

Meenakshi's name, which means "fish-eyed," is derived from the

Tamil words "meen" (fish) and "akshi" (eyes), referring to her large, beautiful eyes that resemble those of a fish. This name not only highlights her physical beauty but also symbolizes her all-seeing, protective nature. As she grew up, Meenakshi displayed extraordinary qualities of courage, strength, and intelligence. Trained in the arts of warfare and governance, she became a formidable warrior and a just ruler, embodying the ideal qualities of a sovereign.

Upon reaching adulthood, Meenakshi ascended the throne of Madurai, succeeding her father. She ruled with wisdom and fairness, bringing prosperity and stability to her kingdom. Her reign is often depicted as a golden age, marked by justice, peace, and the flourishing of arts and culture. Meenakshi's ability to balance her roles as a warrior and a ruler underscores her multifaceted nature and divine origin.

The pivotal moment in Meenakshi's life came when she set out on a military expedition to conquer the world. Her conquests were swift and decisive, and she defeated all who opposed her. Eventually, she reached Mount Kailash, the abode of Shiva, where she encountered the god himself. As prophesied, upon meeting Shiva, her third breast disappeared, signifying the fulfillment of her destiny. Meenakshi realized that Shiva was her divine consort, and their union was ordained by the cosmos.

The marriage of Meenakshi and Shiva is celebrated as a grand event in Hindu mythology, symbolizing the union of divine power and earthly sovereignty. The celestial wedding, known as Meenakshi Thirukalyanam, is commemorated annually in Madurai with great pomp and devotion. This festival, part of the larger Chithirai Festival, draws millions of devotees and tourists to the Meenakshi Amman Temple, one of the most important and magnificent temples in India. The celebrations include elaborate rituals, processions, and cultural performances, reflecting the deep reverence for Meenakshi and her divine consort.

The Meenakshi Amman Temple, located in the heart of Madurai, is a testament to the goddess's enduring legacy and the city's rich cultural heritage. The temple complex, spanning over 14 acres, is a marvel of Dravidian architecture, featuring towering gopurams (gateway towers), intricately carved pillars, and a sacred tank. The temple's central sanctum houses the idols of Meenakshi and Sundareshwarar (Shiva), symbolizing their divine union. Devotees from all over the world visit the temple to seek blessings, offer prayers, and participate in the vibrant rituals and festivals that celebrate the goddess's power and grace.

Meenakshi's role as a warrior queen is particularly significant in a cultural and historical context. In a patriarchal society where female rulers were rare, Meenakshi's story stands out as a powerful narrative of female strength and leadership. Her ability to lead armies, administer justice, and rule a prosperous kingdom challenges traditional gender roles and highlights the potential for women to hold positions of power and authority. Meenakshi's legend serves as an inspiration for women, emphasizing that strength, wisdom, and leadership are not confined to one gender.

The worship of Meenakshi is not limited to her martial prowess but extends to her role as a nurturing and compassionate mother goddess. She is revered as a protector of her devotees, offering solace and support in times of need. The rituals and prayers dedicated to Meenakshi often emphasize her maternal qualities, invoking her blessings for health, prosperity, and well-being. This duality of Meenakshi—as both a fierce warrior and a loving mother—reflects the complexity and depth of the divine feminine in Hinduism.

Meenakshi's influence extends beyond the religious sphere into various aspects of art and culture. Her story has inspired countless works of literature, music, dance, and visual arts. In classical Tamil literature, Meenakshi is celebrated in numerous poems and hymns that praise her beauty, strength, and divinity. The devotional songs dedicated to her, known as Meenakshi Padalgal, are a significant part of Tamil religious and cultural heritage, sung by devotees in temples and during festivals.

In the realm of dance, the story of Meenakshi has been a popular theme in Bharatanatyam, the classical dance form of Tamil Nadu. Dancers depict episodes from her life, portraying her valor, grace, and divine union with Shiva through expressive movements and intricate choreography. These performances not only celebrate the goddess but also serve as a means of preserving and transmitting cultural and religious narratives to future generations.

The visual representation of Meenakshi in temple art, paintings, and sculptures further underscores her importance in Hindu iconography. She is typically depicted as a regal figure, adorned with jewels and royal attire, holding a parrot in one hand and a bouquet of flowers in the other. This imagery symbolizes her beauty, grace, and her connection to nature. The parrot, often associated with Kama, the god of love, signifies Meenakshi's role as a beloved and revered goddess, while the flowers represent fertility and abundance.

Meenakshi's story also highlights the interplay between local traditions and broader Hindu mythology. While she is primarily worshipped in Tamil Nadu, her narrative and symbolism resonate with broader themes in Hinduism, such as the divine feminine, the union of Shiva and Shakti, and the role of the goddess as a protector and nurturer. This interconnectedness reflects the dynamic and inclusive nature of Hinduism, where local deities and traditions are integrated into the larger tapestry of religious and cultural beliefs.

In contemporary times, the legacy of Meenakshi continues to inspire and influence various aspects of life in Madurai and beyond.

Her story serves as a reminder of the enduring power of female leadership and the importance of nurturing and protecting one's community. The values embodied by Meenakshi—strength, wisdom, compassion, and justice—remain relevant and inspiring, offering valuable lessons for individuals and society.

Meenakshi's role as the Queen of Madurai and a divine protector underscores the importance of leadership that is both strong and compassionate. Her example encourages leaders to balance assertiveness with empathy, to administer justice with fairness, and to protect and nurture their communities. This model of leadership is particularly significant in a world where challenges such as inequality, conflict, and environmental degradation require solutions that are both bold and compassionate.

Furthermore, Meenakshi's association with Madurai highlights the importance of cultural heritage and the need to preserve and celebrate historical and religious traditions. The city's identity is closely linked to the goddess, and the preservation of the Meenakshi Amman Temple and its rituals is essential for maintaining the cultural and spiritual vibrancy of the region. Efforts to protect and promote the temple as a UNESCO World Heritage site reflect the recognition of its significance and the need to safeguard it for future generations.

The story of Meenakshi also emphasizes the role of women in religious and cultural narratives. By celebrating female deities and leaders, Hinduism offers a rich and diverse perspective on the divine and human experience. Meenakshi's legend challenges traditional gender roles and highlights the potential for women to embody strength, wisdom, and leadership. Her worship provides a space for women to connect with their own divine potential and to find inspiration in the goddess's example.

Meenakshi, the Queen of Madurai, represents the ideal fusion of divine and royal power, embodying the qualities of strength, beauty, compassion, and wisdom. Her story is a testament to the enduring power of female leadership and the importance of nurturing and protecting one's community. Through her worship, art, literature, and cultural practices, Meenakshi continues to inspire and influence individuals and society, offering valuable lessons on the importance of balance, justice, and compassion in leadership and life. Her legacy as a warrior queen and a benevolent mother goddess underscores the richness and depth of the divine feminine in Hinduism, reminding us of the timeless values that sustain and uplift humanity.

❧❧❧

"Radha, the symbol of divine love, represents the soul's yearning for union with the divine. Her devotion to Krishna teaches us the depth of spiritual love and longing. Through her, we learn the power of unwavering devotion."

TWELVE

KAMAKHYA: THE GODDESS OF DESIRE AND FERTILITY

Kamakhya, the goddess of desire and fertility, holds a unique and powerful position in Hindu mythology and religious practice. She is primarily worshipped in the Kamakhya Temple, located in the Nilachal Hills of Assam, India. Kamakhya's story and symbolism encompass the profound aspects of feminine energy, sexual desire, fertility, and the creative forces of nature. Her worship, deeply rooted in tantric practices, celebrates the sacredness of desire and the cyclical nature of life and fertility. Kamakhya's presence in the spiritual landscape of India underscores the complex and nuanced understanding of the divine feminine in Hinduism.

Kamakhya is often associated with the yoni, the vulva, which is a central symbol in her worship and represents the source of all creation. According to legend, Kamakhya is linked to the story of Sati, the first consort of Shiva. Sati's father, King Daksha, disapproved of her marriage to Shiva and organized a grand yajna (sacrifice) to which he did not invite the couple. Humiliated and distraught, Sati immolated herself in the sacrificial fire. Enraged by her death, Shiva carried Sati's charred body and performed the Tandava, a cosmic dance of destruction. To calm Shiva and prevent further devastation, Vishnu used his Sudarshana Chakra to cut Sati's body into fifty-one pieces, which fell to the earth and became sacred sites known as Shakti Peethas. The yoni of Sati fell on the Nilachal Hill, and the Kamakhya Temple was established at this spot, making it one of the most revered Shakti Peethas.

The Kamakhya Temple, a major pilgrimage site, is unique in its focus on the worship of the yoni. The temple does not contain an idol of the goddess; instead, the sanctum sanctorum houses a natural stone formation shaped like a yoni, symbolizing the creative and generative power of the feminine. The stone is kept moist by a natural spring, emphasizing the theme of fertility and the life-giving properties of water. This focus on the yoni as a sacred symbol highlights the celebration of female sexuality and the acknowledgment of the creative forces inherent in nature.

Kamakhya is revered as the goddess of desire, often associated with the primal forces of nature and the cycles of fertility. Her worship is deeply intertwined with tantric practices, which emphasize the acceptance and transcendence of physical desires as a path to spiritual enlightenment. Tantra views the body and its desires as sacred, and through rituals and meditation, practitioners seek to harmonize the physical and spiritual aspects of existence. Kamakhya, as the embodiment of desire, represents the vital force (Shakti) that drives all creation, urging devotees to embrace their desires and channel them towards spiritual growth.

The Ambubachi Mela, an annual festival held at the Kamakhya Temple, celebrates the goddess's menstruation, symbolizing the fertility of the earth and the creative power of the feminine. During this time, the temple is closed for three days to allow the goddess to rest, and it is believed that the earth becomes especially fertile and potent. On the fourth day, the temple reopens, and devotees are allowed to receive the blessings of the goddess. The festival attracts thousands of pilgrims who come to honor Kamakhya and seek her blessings for fertility, prosperity, and spiritual growth. The celebration of Kamakhya's menstruation underscores the sacredness of the female body and its natural cycles, challenging societal taboos surrounding menstruation and affirming its spiritual significance.

Kamakhya's association with fertility extends beyond human reproduction to encompass the fertility of the land and the cycles of nature. The goddess is often invoked by farmers seeking a bountiful harvest and by couples desiring children. Her blessings are believed to ensure the prosperity and continuity of life, reflecting the interconnectedness of human existence with the natural world. The rituals and offerings dedicated to Kamakhya emphasize the need to honor and respect the forces of nature that sustain life.

The symbolism of Kamakhya also touches on the themes of transformation and regeneration. Just as the cycles of fertility involve periods of dormancy and renewal, the worship of Kamakhya acknowledges the inevitability of change and the potential for rebirth. Her worship encourages devotees to embrace the transformative power of desire and to view challenges and obstacles as opportunities for growth and renewal. This perspective aligns with the tantric philosophy of seeing all aspects of life, including those that are often marginalized or suppressed, as integral to the spiritual journey.

Kamakhya's role as the goddess of desire and fertility also highlights the importance of female agency and empowerment. In a cultural context where women's sexuality and desires have often been restricted or controlled, the worship of Kamakhya offers a space for the celebration and affirmation of female power. The goddess's independent and potent nature serves as a source of inspiration for women to embrace their desires and assert their autonomy. This empowerment is reflected in the temple's rituals, which often involve female priests and practitioners who play a central role in the worship and celebration of the goddess.

The artistic and cultural expressions inspired by Kamakhya further illustrate her significance in the spiritual and cultural life of India. Her story and symbolism have been depicted in various forms of art, literature, and performance. Traditional dance forms like Bharatanatyam and Odissi often include narratives that celebrate Kamakhya's power and grace. Folk songs and devotional hymns praise her as the benevolent mother and the powerful goddess who fulfills the desires of her devotees. These artistic expressions serve not only to honor Kamakhya but also to transmit her teachings and values to future generations.

Kamakhya's influence extends beyond the boundaries of Assam, resonating with devotees and spiritual seekers across India and beyond. Her worship embodies the tantric principles of embracing the physical and the spiritual, the sacred and the mundane, as interconnected aspects of existence. This holistic approach to spirituality challenges dualistic notions that separate body and spirit, desire and purity, and emphasizes the unity of all aspects of life. Kamakhya's teachings encourage a deeper understanding of desire as a natural and powerful force that, when channeled appropriately, can lead to spiritual awakening and fulfillment.

The significance of Kamakhya in contemporary times is particularly relevant in the context of discussions around gender, sexuality, and the empowerment of women. Her worship challenges patriarchal norms and offers a framework for understanding female sexuality as sacred and empowering. The temple's emphasis on the yoni as a symbol of creative power provides a counter-narrative to societal taboos and stigmas associated with female sexuality and menstruation. By honoring Kamakhya, devotees affirm the value and dignity of the female body and its natural functions, promoting a more inclusive and respectful understanding of gender and sexuality.

Kamakhya's story also highlights the importance of ecological awareness and the need to honor and protect the natural world. Her association with the cycles of nature and the fertility of the earth underscores the interconnectedness of human life with the environment. The rituals and festivals dedicated to Kamakhya often include offerings of flowers, fruits, and other natural products, reflecting a deep reverence for the earth and its bounty. This ecological consciousness is particularly relevant in the face of contemporary environmental challenges, reminding us of the need to cultivate a harmonious and sustainable relationship with nature.

The worship of Kamakhya also emphasizes the importance of community and collective celebration. Festivals like the Ambubachi Mela bring together people from diverse backgrounds, fostering a sense of unity and shared purpose. The communal rituals and practices associated with Kamakhya's worship create a space for collective expression and support, reinforcing the bonds of community and the shared commitment to honoring the divine feminine. This sense of community is essential for sustaining the spiritual and cultural traditions associated with Kamakhya and for promoting a more inclusive and compassionate society.

Kamakhya, the goddess of desire and fertility, embodies the profound and transformative power of the feminine divine. Her worship, rooted in tantric practices, celebrates the sacredness of desire and the cycles of fertility that sustain life. The Kamakhya Temple, with its focus on the yoni as a symbol of creative power, challenges societal taboos and affirms the value of female sexuality and agency. Kamakhya's teachings offer a holistic approach to spirituality, emphasizing the unity of physical and spiritual aspects of existence. Her significance in contemporary discussions around gender, sexuality, and ecological awareness highlights the enduring relevance of her story and symbolism. By honoring Kamakhya, devotees affirm the sacredness of desire, the importance of female empowerment, and the need to cultivate a respectful and sustainable relationship with the natural world.

❧❧❧

"Sita, the embodiment of virtue and devotion, exemplifies righteousness and moral integrity. Her life story is a profound lesson in patience and unwavering dedication to dharma. She remains an enduring figure of inspiration and reverence."

THIRTEEN
SANTOSHI MATA: THE MOTHER OF SATISFACTION

Santoshi Mata, the Mother of Satisfaction, is a relatively recent addition to the Hindu pantheon, yet she has quickly become a beloved and widely venerated goddess. Her name, Santoshi, means "contentment" or "satisfaction," reflecting her role as a deity who grants peace, happiness, and contentment to her devotees. The worship of Santoshi Mata, particularly popular among women, highlights themes of familial harmony, personal fulfillment, and spiritual well-being. Her story and the rituals associated with her worship provide insights into the values of devotion, patience, and gratitude.

The origins of Santoshi Mata are somewhat modern compared to other ancient deities, with her widespread worship gaining prominence in the late 20th century. Her rise in popularity is often attributed to the 1975 Bollywood film "Jai Santoshi Maa," which portrayed her as a powerful and compassionate goddess who fulfills the wishes of her devotees. The film's immense success popularized Santoshi Mata across India, leading to the establishment of numerous temples dedicated to her and the widespread observance of rituals and fasts in her honor.

According to the mythological narrative popularized by the film and various folk stories, Santoshi Mata is the daughter of Lord Ganesha, the elephant-headed god of wisdom and remover of obstacles. She is depicted as a kind and benevolent deity who brings joy and satisfaction to those who worship her with devotion and sincerity. The stories often emphasize her ability to resolve familial conflicts, grant prosperity, and ensure the well-being of her devotees. Santoshi Mata's association with Ganesha underscores her role as a remover of obstacles and a provider of happiness and contentment.

The primary ritual associated with Santoshi Mata is the observance of the Santoshi Mata Vrat (fast), which is performed on Fridays. Devotees, particularly women, undertake this fast to seek the goddess's blessings for personal and familial happiness. The ritual involves abstaining from sour and acidic foods, as it is believed that these foods are displeasing to Santoshi Mata. Instead, devotees prepare a simple meal of jaggery (unrefined sugar) and gram (chickpeas) as an offering to the goddess. The fast is typically observed for sixteen consecutive Fridays, during which devotees read or listen to the Santoshi Mata Katha, a narrative that recounts the goddess's virtues, miracles, and the rewards of devotion.

The story often recited during the Santoshi Mata Vrat Katha highlights the transformative power of faith and devotion. It tells of a poor woman who, despite facing numerous hardships and mistreatment from her in-laws, remains steadfast in her devotion to Santoshi Mata. Through her unwavering faith and the observance of the Friday fast, the woman ultimately achieves happiness, prosperity, and harmony in her family. This narrative reinforces the values of patience, perseverance, and the belief that true devotion to the goddess will lead to fulfillment and contentment.

Santoshi Mata's appeal lies in her accessibility and the simplicity of her worship. Unlike some deities whose rituals and worship may involve elaborate ceremonies and extensive knowledge of scriptures, Santoshi Mata can be approached with simple and heartfelt devotion. This accessibility has contributed to her widespread popularity, especially among women from various socio-economic backgrounds. Her worship provides a sense of empowerment and hope, offering devotees a means to overcome their challenges and achieve a sense of satisfaction and peace.

The themes of contentment and gratitude are central to the worship of Santoshi Mata. In a world where desires and aspirations often lead to dissatisfaction and unrest, Santoshi Mata's teachings emphasize the importance of appreciating what one has and finding joy in the present moment. Her blessings are believed to bring not just material prosperity but also a deeper sense of inner peace and fulfillment. This focus on contentment aligns with broader spiritual teachings in Hinduism that advocate for detachment from material desires and the cultivation of a grateful heart.

Santoshi Mata's worship also highlights the significance of family and domestic harmony. Many devotees seek her blessings to resolve conflicts within their families, improve relationships, and ensure the well-being of their loved ones. The goddess's role as a protector of family harmony resonates deeply in a cultural context where familial bonds are highly valued. Her story and rituals reinforce the importance of patience, understanding, and mutual respect in maintaining harmonious relationships.

The rise of Santoshi Mata's worship in the modern era can also be seen as a reflection of the evolving nature of Hindu spirituality. Her relatively recent emergence and rapid acceptance into the Hindu pantheon demonstrate the dynamic and inclusive nature of Hinduism, which continuously evolves to meet the spiritual needs of its followers. Santoshi Mata's story and the simplicity of her worship offer a contemporary model of devotion that resonates with the everyday lives of her devotees, providing a sense of hope and reassurance in times of difficulty.

Temples dedicated to Santoshi Mata have sprung up across India, serving as centers of devotion and community gatherings. These temples are often bustling with activity on Fridays, as devotees come together to perform the Friday fast, offer prayers, and seek the goddess's blessings. The communal aspect of her worship fosters a sense of solidarity and shared faith among devotees, reinforcing the values of community and collective worship.

Santoshi Mata's influence extends beyond religious practices into various cultural expressions. Devotional songs, hymns, and folk stories celebrating her virtues are popular among her followers, contributing to the rich tapestry of Hindu devotional literature and music. These cultural expressions serve to transmit the goddess's teachings and stories to future generations, ensuring the continuity of her worship and the values she embodies.

In contemporary times, the worship of Santoshi Mata holds particular relevance in addressing the challenges of modern life. The fast-paced, consumer-driven society often leads to stress, anxiety, and a constant sense of unfulfillment. Santoshi Mata's teachings of contentment, gratitude, and devotion offer a counterbalance to these pressures, encouraging individuals to find peace and satisfaction within themselves and their relationships. Her worship provides a spiritual framework for navigating the complexities of modern life, promoting mental and emotional well-being through the cultivation of a content and grateful heart.

Moreover, Santoshi Mata's emphasis on simple and sincere devotion resonates with the growing interest in accessible and inclusive spiritual practices. As people seek meaningful ways to connect with the divine and find solace in their daily lives, Santoshi

Mata's worship offers a practical and heartfelt path to spiritual fulfillment. Her teachings remind devotees that true satisfaction comes not from the accumulation of material possessions but from a deep sense of gratitude and inner peace.

The story of Santoshi Mata also underscores the transformative power of faith and the belief that divine intervention can bring about positive change. For many devotees, her worship is a source of hope and inspiration, providing a sense of agency and empowerment in the face of life's challenges. By placing their trust in the goddess and following her teachings, devotees find the strength to overcome obstacles and achieve their aspirations.

Santoshi Mata, the Mother of Satisfaction, embodies the values of contentment, gratitude, and familial harmony. Her worship, characterized by simple and heartfelt devotion, offers a path to inner peace and fulfillment. The story of her rise to prominence and the rituals associated with her worship reflect the dynamic and inclusive nature of Hindu spirituality, which adapts to meet the evolving needs of its followers. In a modern world marked by constant desires and pressures, Santoshi Mata's teachings provide a timeless reminder of the importance of appreciating what one has, nurturing harmonious relationships, and cultivating a grateful heart. Through her blessings, devotees find the strength to navigate life's challenges and achieve a deep sense of satisfaction and well-being.

ppp

"Parvati, the gentle mother and nurturer, embodies love, compassion, and balance. Her devotion and perseverance highlight the importance of nurturing and protecting our loved ones. Through her, we learn the values of resilience and love."

FOURTEEN

CHANDI: THE FIERCE FORM OF SHAKTI

Chandi, the fierce form of Shakti, embodies the raw, unbridled power of the divine feminine. She is one of the most formidable goddesses in Hindu mythology, representing the ferocious aspect of the Goddess who fights against evil and restores cosmic balance. Her story is primarily recounted in the Devi Mahatmya, a text within the Markandeya Purana, which extols her might and valor in battling the forces of darkness. Chandi, also known as Durga or Mahishasuramardini, is a symbol of the triumph of good over evil and the ultimate protector of the universe.

The origins of Chandi are intertwined with the broader narrative of the Goddess, or Devi, in Hindu mythology. The Devi Mahatmya, also known as the Chandi Path or Durga Saptashati, is a seminal text that celebrates the power and glory of the Goddess. It is here that the tale of Chandi unfolds in vivid detail. The text is divided into three sections, each chronicling different battles fought by the Goddess against various demons. Chandi's fierce and unyielding nature is highlighted through these narratives, showcasing her as the ultimate embodiment of Shakti, the divine feminine energy that animates and sustains the cosmos.

One of the most famous and significant stories involving Chandi is her battle with Mahishasura, the buffalo demon. Mahishasura, through intense penance, received a boon from Brahma that made him invincible to any man or god. Empowered by this boon, he waged a war against the gods, driving them out of heaven and causing chaos throughout the universe. The gods, helpless against Mahishasura's might, approached the trinity of Brahma, Vishnu, and Shiva for assistance. In response, the three gods combined their divine energies to create a powerful goddess, Chandi. This formidable form of the Goddess, with her many arms each wielding a divine weapon, was born to defeat Mahishasura and restore order.

Chandi's battle with Mahishasura is a dramatic and awe-inspiring tale that underscores her fearsome power and indomitable spirit. She rides into battle on a lion, symbolizing courage and strength. Her many arms, each holding a weapon given by the gods, signify her ability to combat multiple threats simultaneously. The battle is fierce and prolonged, with Mahishasura shape-shifting into various forms to elude defeat. However, Chandi, with her unparalleled prowess and divine fury, ultimately slays Mahishasura, restoring balance and peace to the universe. This victory is celebrated during the festival of Durga Puja, particularly in Bengal, where the goddess is venerated with great fervor.

The iconography of Chandi is rich with symbolic elements that convey her formidable nature. She is often depicted with a fierce countenance, her eyes blazing with anger and determination. Her hair is usually disheveled, adding to her wild and untamed appearance. The lion she rides symbolizes her mastery over raw power and her fearless nature. The various weapons she holds, such as the trident, sword, discus, and bow, represent her capability to destroy evil in all its forms. Chandi's form is a reminder of the fierce and protective aspect of the divine feminine, capable of immense destruction when necessary to uphold dharma (righteousness).

Chandi's significance extends beyond her martial prowess. She is also a protector of the oppressed and a refuge for those in distress. Her fierce nature is tempered by her compassion for her devotees, who seek her protection and blessings. In times of crisis, believers turn to Chandi, invoking her powerful presence to dispel fear and overcome obstacles. This duality of fierceness and compassion makes her a multifaceted deity, embodying both the nurturing and destructive aspects of the divine feminine.

The worship of Chandi is an integral part of Hindu religious practice, particularly in regions like Bengal, where Durga Puja is a major festival. During this festival, elaborate idols of Chandi as Durga are crafted and worshipped with great devotion. The festivities include rituals, music, dance, and community gatherings, reflecting the deep cultural and spiritual significance of the goddess. The immersion of the idols in water at the end of the festival symbolizes the cyclical nature of creation and destruction, highlighting Chandi's role in the eternal cycle of the cosmos.

The philosophical teachings associated with Chandi emphasize the importance of inner strength and the ability to confront and overcome adversity. Her story inspires individuals to harness their inner power and face challenges with courage and determination. The battles she fights against demons are symbolic of the inner battles each person must wage against their own fears, doubts, and negative tendencies. By invoking Chandi, devotees seek to awaken the fierce and resilient aspects of their own nature, enabling them to navigate life's challenges with confidence and fortitude.

Chandi's role as a warrior goddess also highlights the concept of righteous anger. In Hindu philosophy, anger is generally seen as a negative emotion that can lead to destructive consequences if left unchecked. However, Chandi's anger is righteous and justified, directed against the forces of evil and injustice. This distinction is important, as it underscores the idea that anger, when channeled towards a just cause and controlled by wisdom, can be a powerful force for good. Chandi teaches that it is not anger itself that is harmful, but how it is used and directed.

The story of Chandi also underscores the significance of divine intervention in the battle between good and evil. When the gods are unable to defeat Mahishasura, they turn to the divine feminine for assistance, acknowledging the superior power of Shakti. This narrative reinforces the idea that the feminine principle is not subordinate but rather essential and central to the cosmic order. Chandi's intervention is a testament to the indispensable role of the divine feminine in maintaining balance and harmony in the universe.

Chandi's worship is not confined to India; her influence extends to various parts of the world where Hinduism has spread. Temples dedicated to the goddess can be found in Nepal, Bangladesh, and other regions with significant Hindu populations. Her fierce yet protective nature resonates with devotees across cultural and geographical boundaries, making her a universally revered figure in the Hindu diaspora.

The cultural and artistic expressions inspired by Chandi are vast and varied. Her story has been depicted in countless forms of art, including sculpture, painting, dance, and theater. In traditional Indian dance forms like Bharatanatyam and Kathak, performances often include narratives that celebrate Chandi's valor and victories. These performances not only honor the goddess but also serve as a means of transmitting her stories and teachings to future generations.

Literature and poetry dedicated to Chandi, particularly in the form of hymns and devotional songs, play a crucial role in her worship. Texts like the Chandi Path and Durga Saptashati are recited during festivals and rituals, invoking the goddess's presence and blessings.

These recitations are believed to purify the environment, dispel negative energies, and invoke the protective power of the goddess.

Chandi's story also offers valuable lessons for contemporary society. Her fierce defense of righteousness and protection of the oppressed can inspire individuals and communities to stand against injustice and fight for what is right. In a world where inequities and challenges abound, Chandi's example serves as a powerful reminder of the importance of resilience, courage, and the willingness to confront and overcome adversity.

Moreover, Chandi's embodiment of Shakti underscores the significance of female empowerment and the recognition of the divine feminine's vital role. Her story challenges patriarchal norms and highlights the strength, wisdom, and capability of women. By celebrating Chandi, devotees acknowledge and honor the powerful and protective aspects of femininity, promoting a more inclusive and equitable understanding of gender roles.

Chandi, the fierce form of Shakti, represents the indomitable power and protective nature of the divine feminine. Her story, celebrated in texts like the Devi Mahatmya, highlights her role as the ultimate warrior who defeats evil and restores cosmic balance. Through her worship, devotees seek to invoke her strength, courage, and protective blessings. Chandi's significance extends beyond mythology, offering profound philosophical insights and practical lessons for navigating life's challenges. Her fierce yet compassionate nature embodies the dual aspects of the divine feminine, inspiring resilience, righteous action, and the recognition of the vital role of Shakti in the universe. Through the celebration of Chandi, the fierce form of Shakti, the timeless values of courage, justice, and the protective power of the divine feminine are honored and upheld.

ppp

"Kali, the fierce protector and destroyer, represents the transformative power of facing fears and challenges. Her fearsome appearance symbolizes the raw energy of the divine. She teaches us to embrace our shadow selves for true transformation."

FIFTEEN

BHUMI: THE EARTH GODDESS

Bhumi, the Earth Goddess, is a central figure in Hindu mythology, symbolizing the nurturing and sustaining aspects of the Earth. As the personification of the planet, Bhumi embodies the qualities of fertility, stability, and nourishment. Her role is vital in the cosmic order, providing the foundation upon which life thrives. Bhumi's significance extends beyond her mythological attributes, reflecting the deep cultural and spiritual connection between humans and the Earth. She is revered not only as a divine entity but also as the physical and spiritual ground that supports all existence.

In Hindu cosmology, Bhumi is often depicted as a benevolent and nurturing mother, emphasizing her role as the provider and sustainer of life. She is frequently portrayed as a beautiful woman seated on a lotus, symbolizing purity and the interconnectedness of all life forms.

In her hands, she holds a pot of herbs and a pomegranate, representing fertility, abundance, and the healing properties of the Earth. This imagery underscores her role in agriculture and medicine, essential aspects of human survival and well-being.

One of the most prominent myths associated with Bhumi is her role in the Ramayana, where she is depicted as the mother of Sita, the wife of Lord Rama. According to the epic, Sita was found as an infant in a furrow by King Janaka while he was plowing the fields. This miraculous birth connects Sita directly to Bhumi, highlighting the Earth's role as a life-giving force.

Sita's eventual return to the Earth, when she seeks refuge in her mother after enduring years of hardship, further reinforces the bond between Bhumi and her children, symbolizing the ultimate return to one's origins.

Bhumi is also deeply integrated into the narrative of Vishnu, one of the principal deities in Hinduism. She is considered an incarnation of the goddess Lakshmi, Vishnu's consort, in her form as Bhudevi. In various myths, Bhumi is depicted alongside Vishnu, where she plays a crucial role in the sustenance of the universe.
In the Varaha avatar, one of Vishnu's ten incarnations, he rescues Bhumi, who had been submerged in the cosmic ocean by the demon Hiranyaksha. Vishnu, in the form of a boar, dives into the ocean, lifts Bhumi on his tusks, and restores her to her rightful place. This myth highlights Bhumi's vulnerability and the divine intervention necessary to protect and sustain her.

The worship of Bhumi is integral to various agricultural practices in India. Farmers and cultivators pay homage to her before sowing seeds and during harvest festivals, seeking her blessings for a bountiful yield. These rituals, often performed at the onset of the monsoon season, reflect the deep reverence for the Earth and the recognition of her essential role in providing sustenance.

Festivals such as Pongal in Tamil Nadu, Makar Sankranti in various parts of India, and Baisakhi in Punjab celebrate the Earth's fertility and the cyclical nature of life. These celebrations are marked by communal prayers, offerings of the first produce, and various cultural activities that honor Bhumi's generosity.

Bhumi's role extends beyond agricultural significance to include environmental stewardship and the preservation of nature. In Hindu philosophy, the Earth is not merely a resource to be exploited but a living entity that must be respected and protected.

This perspective is encapsulated in the concept of "Prithvi Sukta," a hymn from the Atharva Veda, which extols the virtues of the Earth and calls for her protection and sustainable use. The hymn praises the Earth for her bounty and calls upon humans to live in harmony with her, emphasizing the need for ecological balance and respect for all living beings.

The relationship between humans and Bhumi is also explored in various Puranic texts, where she is depicted as a compassionate and nurturing mother who responds to the needs and sufferings of her children. In these narratives, Bhumi is often shown intervening in human affairs, either directly or through her divine offspring, to restore balance and justice.

For instance, in the Mahabharata, Bhumi plays a significant role in the tale of Narakasura, a demon who oppressed the Earth and her inhabitants. Bhumi appeals to Vishnu, who incarnates as Krishna, to defeat Narakasura and liberate the Earth from his tyranny. This story underscores the interconnectedness of divine intervention, human actions, and the well-being of the Earth.

Bhumi's significance is also reflected in various architectural and artistic traditions in India. Temples dedicated to her, though not as numerous as those for other deities, can be found in different parts of the country. These temples often feature intricate carvings and sculptures that depict her in her various forms and highlight her importance in the Hindu pantheon. The artistic representations of Bhumi in temple architecture and iconography serve as a reminder of her enduring presence and the reverence accorded to her by devotees.

In contemporary times, Bhumi's symbolism has taken on new dimensions, particularly in the context of environmental conservation and sustainable development. As the world faces increasing ecological challenges, the worship of Bhumi serves as a powerful reminder of the need to protect and preserve the Earth. Environmental activists and spiritual leaders often invoke Bhumi in their efforts to promote ecological awareness and advocate for sustainable practices. Her representation as the nurturing Earth Mother resonates with contemporary concerns about climate change, deforestation, pollution, and the depletion of natural resources.

The modern environmental movement in India has drawn inspiration from traditional beliefs and practices associated with Bhumi. Initiatives such as tree planting, river cleaning, and the promotion of organic farming are often undertaken with a sense of reverence for Bhumi and the recognition of her central role in sustaining life. These efforts highlight the need to reconnect with ancient wisdom and practices that emphasize living in harmony with nature. By invoking Bhumi, contemporary environmentalists seek to foster a sense of stewardship and responsibility towards the Earth, encouraging communities to protect and nurture the environment for future generations.

Bhumi's teachings also extend to the realm of social justice and equity. The Earth, as a common heritage of all humanity, must be shared and protected in a manner that ensures fairness and justice. This perspective aligns with the principles of "Vasudhaiva Kutumbakam," a Sanskrit phrase that means "the world is one family." By recognizing the interconnectedness of all life and the shared responsibility to protect the Earth, Bhumi's worship promotes values of inclusivity, compassion, and collective action.

This approach advocates for the equitable distribution of resources and the protection of marginalized communities who are often disproportionately affected by environmental degradation.

The worship of Bhumi also emphasizes the importance of mindfulness and gratitude in everyday life. By acknowledging the Earth as a living entity and expressing gratitude for her gifts, individuals can cultivate a deeper sense of connection and respect for the natural world. Practices such as mindful consumption, reducing waste, and conserving resources are ways to honor Bhumi and contribute to her well-being. This mindful approach to living encourages individuals to reflect on their impact on the Earth and to make choices that support sustainability and ecological balance.

The symbolism of Bhumi also finds resonance in various cultural and literary traditions. Poets, writers, and artists have long drawn inspiration from the Earth and her attributes, creating works that celebrate her beauty, resilience, and nurturing qualities. These cultural expressions serve to reinforce the reverence for Bhumi and the recognition of her essential role in human life. Through literature, art, and music, the stories and teachings of Bhumi are transmitted across generations, fostering a deep and abiding connection with the Earth.

Bhumi, the Earth Goddess, represents the foundational and nurturing aspects of the Earth, embodying qualities of fertility, stability, and sustenance. Her significance in Hindu mythology, religious practices, and cultural traditions underscores the deep reverence for the Earth and the recognition of her central role in supporting life. The worship of Bhumi highlights the interconnectedness of all life forms and the importance of living in harmony with nature. As contemporary challenges such as climate change and environmental degradation intensify, Bhumi's teachings offer valuable insights into the need for ecological stewardship, social justice, and mindful living. By honoring Bhumi, individuals and communities are reminded of their shared responsibility to protect and nurture the Earth, ensuring her health and vitality for future generations. Through her enduring presence and the values she embodies, Bhumi continues to inspire and guide efforts to create a sustainable and equitable world.

"Saraswati, the goddess of wisdom and learning, encourages the pursuit of knowledge and creativity. Her teachings promote the integration of intellectual and artistic talents. She inspires us to seek enlightenment through education and cultural enrichment."

SIXTEEN

GAYATRI: THE PERSONIFICATION OF THE VEDIC HYMN

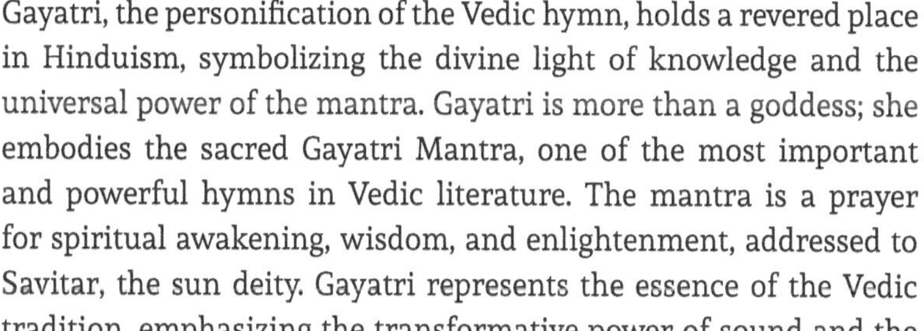

Gayatri, the personification of the Vedic hymn, holds a revered place in Hinduism, symbolizing the divine light of knowledge and the universal power of the mantra. Gayatri is more than a goddess; she embodies the sacred Gayatri Mantra, one of the most important and powerful hymns in Vedic literature. The mantra is a prayer for spiritual awakening, wisdom, and enlightenment, addressed to Savitar, the sun deity. Gayatri represents the essence of the Vedic tradition, emphasizing the transformative power of sound and the importance of meditation and devotion in the pursuit of higher knowledge.

The Gayatri Mantra is found in the Rigveda, one of the oldest and most sacred texts of Hinduism. The mantra is composed in the Gayatri meter, a poetic structure consisting of three lines with eight syllables each. The mantra is as follows:

"Om Bhur Bhuvah Swah,

Tat Savitur Varenyam,

Bhargo Devasya Dheemahi,

Dhiyo Yo Nah Prachodayat."

This translates to: "We meditate on the divine light of the creator; may it inspire our thoughts and guide our intellect."

The Gayatri Mantra is considered the mother of all Vedic mantras, encapsulating the essence of the Vedas. It is a universal prayer that transcends sectarian boundaries and is recited by devotees seeking spiritual growth and enlightenment. The mantra's invocation of Savitar, the sun deity, symbolizes the source of all life and energy, illuminating the path of knowledge and dispelling the darkness of ignorance.

Gayatri, as the personification of this mantra, is depicted as a beautiful goddess with five faces and ten arms, seated on a red lotus. Each of her faces represents a different aspect of knowledge and the five elements (earth, water, fire, air, and ether). Her ten arms hold various symbolic objects, such as the conch, discus, lotus, and book, signifying her multifaceted nature and her role as the bestower of wisdom and enlightenment. The red lotus on which she is seated represents purity and the awakening of the soul through spiritual practice.

The worship of Gayatri as a goddess and the recitation of the Gayatri Mantra are central to the daily spiritual practices of many Hindus. The mantra is traditionally chanted during the Sandhyavandanam, a ritual performed at dawn, noon, and dusk, aligning the practitioner with the cycles of the sun and the natural rhythms of the universe. This practice emphasizes the importance of regular meditation and devotion in cultivating spiritual awareness and inner peace.

Gayatri's significance extends beyond her association with the mantra. She is also regarded as the mother of the Vedas and the embodiment of the divine feminine power that sustains the cosmos. In this role, she is identified with Saraswati, the goddess of wisdom and learning, and Savitri, the goddess of life and energy. This multifaceted identity underscores Gayatri's importance as a source of spiritual illumination and a guiding force in the quest for knowledge.

The transformative power of the Gayatri Mantra lies in its sound vibrations and the meditative focus it cultivates. The repetition of the mantra is believed to purify the mind, enhance concentration, and elevate consciousness. The sound "Om," with which the mantra begins, is the primordial sound, representing the essence of the universe and the ultimate reality. The subsequent words and phrases invoke the divine light and its ability to inspire and guide the intellect, promoting clarity, wisdom, and spiritual growth.

The Gayatri Mantra's emphasis on intellectual and spiritual enlightenment is particularly relevant in the context of the Vedic tradition, which values knowledge and self-realization as the highest goals of human life. The mantra's invocation of the divine light reflects the Vedic belief in the interconnectedness of all life and the pursuit of truth and understanding as a path to liberation. By meditating on the mantra, practitioners seek to align their thoughts and actions with the higher principles of dharma (righteousness) and cosmic order.

The role of Gayatri in the educational and spiritual development of individuals is also significant. In many Hindu traditions, the recitation of the Gayatri Mantra is an essential part of the

Upanayana, the sacred thread ceremony that marks the initiation of young boys into spiritual and academic life. This rite of passage symbolizes the transition from childhood to adulthood and the beginning of a disciplined and purposeful life dedicated to learning and spiritual practice. The Gayatri Mantra, taught to the initiate by the guru, serves as a spiritual guide and a source of inspiration throughout their life.

Gayatri's influence extends to various cultural and philosophical dimensions of Hinduism. She embodies the principle of Shakti, the dynamic and creative energy that underlies the universe. As a manifestation of Shakti, Gayatri represents the active and transformative power of the divine feminine, which brings forth creation, sustains life, and guides the soul towards enlightenment. This understanding of Gayatri highlights the integral role of the feminine principle in the spiritual and material realms, emphasizing the balance and harmony between different aspects of existence.

The philosophical teachings associated with Gayatri also underscore the importance of inner transformation and the cultivation of virtues. The mantra's invocation of divine light and wisdom encourages practitioners to develop qualities such as clarity, discernment, compassion, and humility. By aligning their thoughts and actions with these higher principles, individuals can overcome ignorance and delusion, leading to a more harmonious and fulfilling life. Gayatri's teachings remind us that true knowledge is not merely intellectual but involves a holistic understanding of oneself and the world, integrating both heart and mind.

The cultural expressions of Gayatri's worship are diverse and vibrant. Temples dedicated to Gayatri can be found across India, where devotees gather to perform rituals, chant the mantra, and seek the goddess's blessings. Festivals and ceremonies celebrating Gayatri, such as Gayatri Jayanti, are observed with great devotion and enthusiasm, reflecting the deep reverence for the goddess and the mantra she personifies. These celebrations often include recitations of the Gayatri Mantra, homas (sacred fire rituals), and various forms of artistic expression, such as music, dance, and drama, that honor the goddess and her significance.

Gayatri's role in contemporary spiritual practice is particularly noteworthy. In an age characterized by rapid technological advancements and material pursuits, the teachings of Gayatri offer a counterbalance, emphasizing the importance of spiritual growth and inner peace. The practice of reciting the Gayatri Mantra provides a means of reconnecting with one's inner self and the universal principles that sustain life. This focus on meditation and mindfulness helps individuals navigate the complexities of modern life with greater clarity and equanimity.

Furthermore, Gayatri's teachings have inspired various modern spiritual movements and organizations that promote the mantra's practice and the values it embodies. One such movement is the Gayatri Pariwar, founded by Pandit Shriram Sharma Acharya, which aims to spread the message of the Gayatri Mantra and its transformative potential. The organization emphasizes the importance of self-discipline, ethical living, and social service as pathways to individual and collective well-being. Through educational programs, publications, and community initiatives, the Gayatri Pariwar seeks to foster a culture of peace, harmony, and spiritual awakening.

The universal appeal of the Gayatri Mantra and its underlying principles also transcend cultural and religious boundaries. People from diverse backgrounds and spiritual traditions have embraced the mantra for its simplicity, profundity, and transformative power. The mantra's emphasis on the light of knowledge and the quest for truth resonates with universal human aspirations, making it a valuable spiritual tool for individuals seeking inner growth and enlightenment.

Gayatri's significance as the personification of the Vedic hymn underscores the enduring relevance of ancient wisdom in contemporary times. Her teachings remind us of the importance of seeking higher knowledge, cultivating virtues, and aligning our lives with the universal principles of truth and righteousness. By meditating on the Gayatri Mantra and invoking the goddess's blessings, individuals can tap into the transformative power of sound and the divine light, fostering spiritual growth and inner peace.

Gayatri, the personification of the Vedic hymn, embodies the divine light of knowledge and the universal power of the mantra. As the essence of the Gayatri Mantra, she represents the pursuit of spiritual awakening, wisdom, and enlightenment. Her teachings emphasize the transformative potential of meditation and devotion, encouraging individuals to align their thoughts and actions with higher principles. Gayatri's influence extends to various cultural, philosophical, and spiritual dimensions, highlighting the importance of inner transformation and the cultivation of virtues. Through her enduring presence and the practice of the Gayatri Mantra, devotees are guided towards a path of clarity, compassion, and spiritual fulfillment.

ᖾᖾᖾ

"Lakshmi, the bestower of wealth and prosperity, embodies abundance and fortune. Her presence reminds us of the importance of gratitude and ethical living. Through her, we seek prosperity and well-being with humility and generosity."

SEVENTEEN
MANASA: THE SERPENT GODDESS OF FERTILITY AND HEALTH

Manasa, the serpent goddess of fertility and health, holds a unique and powerful place in Hindu mythology, particularly in Bengal, Assam, and other regions of eastern India. As a deity associated with snakes, she embodies both the protective and potentially dangerous aspects of these creatures. Manasa is revered for her ability to cure snakebites, promote fertility, and bring prosperity and health to her devotees. Her story is one of resilience and determination, reflecting her journey from a marginalized figure to a widely venerated goddess.

Manasa's origins are deeply rooted in ancient folklore and rural traditions. She is often described as the daughter of the sage Kashyapa and Kadru, making her the sister of the serpent king Vasuki and other nagas (serpent deities). However, some legends also describe her as a manifestation of Shakti, the divine feminine energy, emphasizing her divine nature and significant power.

Manasa's association with snakes, creatures that are both revered and feared, underscores her dual role as a healer and protector, as well as a figure capable of wielding immense power.

One of the central myths associated with Manasa is her struggle for recognition and acceptance among the gods and humans. According to legend, Manasa sought the devotion of the people and a place among the deities. However, her journey was fraught with challenges, particularly from her stepmother, the goddess Chandi, and her half-brother, Vasuki, who were initially hostile towards her. Despite these obstacles, Manasa's determination and resilience eventually earned her a place of honor. Her persistence in overcoming these trials highlights her role as a goddess who understands suffering and adversity, making her a compassionate and accessible deity for her devotees.

Manasa is particularly revered for her power to cure snakebites, a common and serious danger in rural areas. The fear of snakes and the potentially fatal consequences of snakebites have made her worship crucial for many communities. Devotees seek her protection and blessings to avoid snakebites and to heal those who have been bitten. Manasa's ability to control snakes and her knowledge of antidotes position her as a vital figure in ensuring the safety and well-being of her followers. Her worship often involves rituals and offerings that seek to appease snakes and invoke the goddess's protective powers.

The rituals dedicated to Manasa are deeply symbolic and reflect her dual nature. One of the key rituals involves the installation of a clay or metal image of the goddess, often depicted holding snakes in her hands or surrounded by them. This image is placed in homes or fields to protect against snakebites and ensure fertility and prosperity. Devotees offer milk, flowers, and other items to these images, symbolizing their respect and reverence for the goddess and her serpent companions.

Manasa's association with fertility extends beyond her protective role against snakes. She is also invoked for her blessings in matters of fertility, childbirth, and overall health. In agricultural communities, her blessings are sought to ensure a bountiful harvest and the well-being of livestock. The snake, a symbol of regeneration and renewal due to its ability to shed its skin, further reinforces Manasa's connection to fertility and the cyclical nature of life. Her worship often includes prayers and rituals aimed at promoting the health and prosperity of families and communities.

The festivals dedicated to Manasa, particularly the Manasa Puja, are vibrant and significant events in the regions where she is worshipped. These festivals typically take place during the monsoon season, a time when snakes are more active, and the risk of snakebites is higher. During these celebrations, devotees come together to honor the goddess through songs, dances, and various rituals. The atmosphere is one of communal devotion and celebration, reflecting the deep cultural significance of Manasa's worship and the collective hope for her protection and blessings.

Manasa's worship is also intertwined with the practice of folk healing and medicine. Traditional healers, known as ojhas or snake charmers, often invoke Manasa in their healing practices, particularly in treating snakebites. These healers are believed to possess knowledge of ancient remedies and antidotes, passed down through generations, and they call upon the goddess to aid in their healing efforts. This connection between Manasa and folk medicine underscores her role as a guardian of health and well-being and highlights the integration of religious and practical approaches to health in traditional communities.

The cultural and literary expressions of Manasa's story and worship are rich and varied. The Manasa Mangal, a collection of Bengali narrative poems, is one of the most important texts that celebrate her life and deeds. Composed between the 13th and 18th centuries, these poems recount Manasa's struggles, victories, and the miracles she performed for her devotees. The Manasa Mangal is not only a religious text but also a significant work of literature that reflects the social and cultural contexts of its time. Through these stories, the values and beliefs associated with Manasa are transmitted to future generations, ensuring the continuity of her worship and the preservation of her legacy.

The worship of Manasa also reflects broader themes in Hinduism, such as the importance of resilience, the power of devotion, and the interplay between humans and the natural world. Her story emphasizes the virtues of persistence and determination, illustrating how even a marginalized figure can achieve recognition and reverence through unwavering devotion and effort. This narrative resonates with the experiences of many devotees who face challenges and adversities in their own lives, making Manasa a relatable and inspiring figure.

Furthermore, Manasa's connection to the natural world, particularly through her association with snakes, highlights the reverence for nature that is integral to Hindu spirituality. Her worship underscores the belief that all creatures, even those that are feared or misunderstood, have a place in the cosmic order and deserve respect and protection. This perspective fosters a sense of harmony with the natural world and encourages the responsible and compassionate treatment of all living beings.

In contemporary times, the worship of Manasa continues to be relevant, particularly in rural areas where the threat of snakebites remains a significant concern. However, her influence extends beyond these traditional contexts, resonating with modern environmental and health concerns. The values embodied by Manasa, such as the importance of health, the need for environmental stewardship, and the power of resilience, are increasingly relevant in addressing contemporary challenges. Her story and worship offer insights into how traditional beliefs and practices can inform and enrich modern approaches to health, well-being, and environmental conservation.

Manasa's significance is also reflected in various forms of art and performance. Traditional folk theater, music, and dance often incorporate her story and themes, bringing her legend to life for audiences. These performances serve not only as entertainment but also as a means of educating and inspiring communities, reinforcing the values and beliefs associated with the goddess. Through these cultural expressions, Manasa's legacy continues to thrive, adapting to changing times while preserving the core elements of her worship and significance.

Manasa, the serpent goddess of fertility and health, embodies the dual aspects of protection and danger, nurturing and destruction, that characterize the natural world. Her worship reflects a deep reverence for the power and mystery of snakes, as well as a recognition of their vital role in the ecosystem. As a healer and protector, Manasa offers solace and support to her devotees, guiding them through the challenges of life and promoting their well-being. Her story, rich in symbolism and cultural significance, underscores the importance of resilience, devotion, and harmony with nature. Through her enduring presence and the values she embodies, Manasa continues to inspire and guide individuals and communities, offering a timeless reminder of the interconnectedness of all life and the power of faith and determination.

ॐॐॐ

"Vindhyavasini, the guardian of the Vindhya Range, embodies the power and majesty of nature. Her worship reflects a deep respect for the natural world. She teaches us the importance of living in harmony with the environment."

EIGHTEEN

LALITA: THE GODDESS OF BLISS AND BEAUTY

Lalita, the goddess of bliss and beauty, is one of the most exalted deities in the Hindu pantheon. She is a central figure in the Shakta tradition, which focuses on the worship of the divine feminine. Lalita, also known as Lalita Tripura Sundari, embodies the essence of beauty, grace, and bliss. She is revered as the supreme goddess who transcends all dualities and represents the ultimate reality, combining power, wisdom, and beauty. Her worship, steeped in the rich tapestry of Tantric and Vedic traditions, celebrates the divine feminine's transformative power and the pursuit of spiritual bliss.

Lalita's story is intricately detailed in the Lalita Sahasranama, a sacred text that enumerates her thousand names, each highlighting a different aspect of her divine nature. This text, part of the Brahmanda Purana, is recited by devotees to invoke the goddess's blessings and connect with her divine energy. The Lalita Sahasranama portrays her as the universal mother, the source of all creation, and the embodiment of compassion and love. She is depicted as seated on a throne of the five elements, holding various weapons and symbols that signify her power and dominion over the cosmos.

One of the most important myths associated with Lalita is her battle against the demon Bhandasura. According to legend, Bhandasura was created from the ashes of Kamadeva, the god of love, who was incinerated by Shiva's third eye. Bhandasura, endowed with immense power, terrorized the gods and disrupted the cosmic order. In response, the gods invoked Lalita, who manifested in a resplendent form, radiating beauty and grace. Riding a chariot drawn by swans and accompanied by an army of celestial beings, Lalita engaged Bhandasura in a fierce battle. Using her divine weapons and wisdom, she vanquished the demon and restored harmony to the universe. This narrative underscores Lalita's role as a protector and restorer of cosmic balance, emphasizing her strength and benevolence.

Lalita's iconography is rich with symbolism, reflecting her multifaceted nature. She is often depicted as a youthful and enchanting goddess, exuding an aura of serenity and joy. Her form is adorned with exquisite jewelry and garments, symbolizing her connection to beauty and prosperity. In her four hands, she holds a noose, a goad, a sugarcane bow, and five arrows made of flowers, each representing different aspects of her power. The noose symbolizes her ability to bind and control, the goad represents her power to remove obstacles, the sugarcane bow signifies her control over desire, and the flower arrows denote the sensory pleasures and their ultimate transcendence. These attributes highlight Lalita's dominion over both the material and spiritual realms, as well as her role in guiding devotees towards spiritual liberation.

The worship of Lalita is deeply embedded in Tantric practices, which emphasize the union of the individual soul with the divine. Tantric rituals dedicated to Lalita often involve elaborate ceremonies, mantras, and meditative practices designed to awaken the kundalini energy within the practitioner. This energy, represented as a coiled serpent at the base of the spine, is believed to rise through the chakras, leading to spiritual enlightenment and union with the divine. Lalita, as the supreme goddess, is seen as the guiding force in this transformative journey, helping devotees navigate the path of self-realization and ultimate bliss.

One of the most revered hymns dedicated to Lalita is the Lalita Trishati, which contains 300 names of the goddess, each name encapsulating her divine attributes and powers. Reciting this hymn is believed to invoke her blessings, bestow spiritual knowledge, and bring peace and prosperity to the devotee. The repetition of her names serves as a meditative practice, helping the practitioner focus their mind and connect with the goddess on a deeper level. This practice underscores the importance of devotion and the power of sound vibrations in the worship of Lalita.

Lalita's significance extends beyond her role as a warrior and protector. She is also revered as the goddess of beauty and bliss, embodying the aesthetic and sensory pleasures that elevate the human experience. In the arts, particularly in classical Indian music and dance, Lalita is celebrated as the muse who inspires creativity and expression. Her grace and beauty are often depicted in performances and compositions, which seek to capture the essence of her divine presence. Through these artistic expressions, devotees are able to experience a glimpse of the bliss and transcendence that Lalita represents.

The festival of Navaratri, dedicated to the worship of the goddess in her various forms, includes special observances and rituals in honor of Lalita. During these nine nights, devotees engage in prayers, fasting, and cultural performances to celebrate the divine feminine and seek the goddess's blessings. The fifth day of Navaratri, known as Lalita Panchami, is specifically devoted to Lalita. On this day, elaborate pujas are performed, and devotees chant the Lalita Sahasranama and other hymns to invoke her presence and grace. This festival highlights the communal aspect of Lalita's worship, bringing people together in a shared celebration of the goddess's power and benevolence.

Lalita's worship also encompasses the principles of non-dualism, or Advaita, which emphasize the oneness of the individual soul and the supreme consciousness. In this philosophical framework, Lalita is seen as the embodiment of the ultimate reality, transcending all distinctions and dualities. Her form and attributes are considered manifestations of the divine energy that pervades the universe. By meditating on Lalita and her various aspects, devotees aim to transcend the illusion of separateness and realize their inherent unity with the divine. This realization is seen as the pinnacle of spiritual attainment, bringing about a state of eternal bliss and liberation.

In contemporary times, Lalita's teachings and the practices associated with her worship continue to resonate with spiritual seekers around the world. Her emphasis on inner beauty, grace, and the pursuit of bliss offers a counterbalance to the materialistic values that often dominate modern life. By focusing on the divine feminine and the transformative power of devotion, practitioners are able to cultivate a sense of inner peace and fulfillment. Lalita's worship encourages individuals to embrace the beauty and joy inherent in life, while also striving for higher spiritual goals.

The universality of Lalita's message is reflected in the diverse ways she is revered and celebrated. Her worship transcends cultural and geographical boundaries, resonating with people from various backgrounds and spiritual traditions. The principles of love, beauty, and bliss that she embodies are universal values that speak to the core of the human experience. Through her teachings, Lalita inspires a deeper appreciation for the interconnectedness of all life and the pursuit of harmony and balance in the world.

The integration of Lalita's worship into daily life is also significant. Devotees are encouraged to see the goddess in all aspects of creation, recognizing the divine presence in themselves and others. This perspective fosters a sense of respect and reverence for all beings, promoting a compassionate and holistic approach to life. By embodying the qualities of Lalita—beauty, grace, and bliss—practitioners aim to elevate their own consciousness and contribute positively to the world around them.

Lalita, the goddess of bliss and beauty, represents the highest ideals of the divine feminine in Hinduism. Her story and attributes highlight her role as a protector, guide, and source of inspiration for her devotees. Through her worship, practitioners seek to connect with the divine energy that she embodies, experiencing the transformative power of devotion and the pursuit of spiritual bliss. Lalita's teachings emphasize the importance of inner beauty, grace, and the realization of one's unity with the divine. Her enduring presence in the hearts and minds of devotees continues to inspire and uplift, offering a path to ultimate bliss and spiritual fulfillment.

"Radha's love for Krishna is a divine allegory of the soul's journey toward spiritual enlightenment. Her intense longing and devotion symbolize the pursuit of ultimate union with the divine. She inspires us to seek deeper spiritual connections."

NINETEEN
VINDHYAVASINI: THE MOUNTAIN DWELLING GODDESS

Vindhyavasini, the mountain-dwelling goddess, holds a revered and significant place in Hindu mythology and religious practices. She is particularly venerated in the Vindhya Range, a mountain range in central India that forms a natural boundary between northern and southern India. Vindhyavasini, an incarnation of the goddess Durga, is worshipped for her power, protection, and the blessings she bestows upon her devotees. Her story is deeply embedded in the cultural and spiritual life of the region, reflecting the profound connection between the divine and the natural world.

Vindhyavasini is often depicted as a fierce and benevolent goddess, embodying the qualities of strength, courage, and compassion. She is usually shown riding a lion, symbolizing her power and dominion over the natural and supernatural realms. In her hands, she holds various weapons, including a trident, sword, and discus, signifying her ability to vanquish evil and protect her devotees. Her iconography emphasizes her role as a warrior goddess, ever ready to combat the forces of darkness and uphold righteousness.

The origin of Vindhyavasini is closely linked to the legend of the Vindhya Range and the story of the demon Mahishasura. According to Hindu mythology, Mahishasura, a powerful demon with the ability to transform into a buffalo, performed intense penance to gain a boon from Brahma. He became invincible to all men and gods, leading him to wage war against the heavens and spread terror across the universe. In response to the prayers of the gods, the supreme goddess Durga was invoked to defeat the demon. Durga manifested in various forms, one of which was Vindhyavasini, to defeat Mahishasura and restore cosmic order.

The Vindhya Range itself holds great significance in Hindu cosmology. It is believed to be a powerful and sacred landscape, imbued with the presence of divine energy. Vindhyavasini, as the presiding deity of this region, is thought to embody the spirit and strength of the mountains. The natural environment of the Vindhya Range, with its rugged terrain and dense forests, mirrors the goddess's fierce and protective nature. This association highlights the intimate relationship between the divine and the natural world, where the mountains serve as both a sanctuary and a source of power for the goddess.

The Vindhyavasini Temple, located in the town of Vindhyachal in Uttar Pradesh, is one of the most important pilgrimage sites dedicated to the goddess. Thousands of devotees visit the temple each year, particularly during the Navaratri festival, to seek Vindhyavasini's blessings and protection. The temple, situated on the banks of the holy river Ganges, is a focal point of worship and community activity. The vibrant and bustling atmosphere of the temple during festivals reflects the deep devotion and reverence that devotees have for Vindhyavasini.

Navaratri, the nine-night festival dedicated to the worship of the divine feminine, is a particularly significant time for the worship of Vindhyavasini. During this festival, the goddess is honored with elaborate rituals, prayers, and cultural performances. Devotees observe fasts, chant hymns, and participate in processions to celebrate the goddess's power and grace. The festival culminates in the immersion of the goddess's idol in the river, symbolizing her return to the natural world and the cyclical nature of life and divinity.

The rituals and practices associated with the worship of Vindhyavasini are rich with symbolism and meaning. One of the key rituals is the offering of coconut, fruits, and flowers to the goddess, symbolizing purity, devotion, and the desire for her blessings. Devotees often light oil lamps and incense sticks, creating an atmosphere of reverence and sanctity. The chanting of mantras and hymns dedicated to Vindhyavasini is believed to invoke her presence and invoke her protective and benevolent energies.

Vindhyavasini's worship is not limited to the temple; it extends to the homes and lives of her devotees. Many families maintain small altars dedicated to the goddess, where daily prayers and offerings are made. These domestic practices reflect the personal and intimate relationship that devotees have with Vindhyavasini, viewing her as a guardian and benefactor who watches over them and their families. The goddess's presence in the household is seen as a source of strength and protection, ensuring the well-being and prosperity of the family.

The story of Vindhyavasini also highlights the themes of resilience and perseverance. Her manifestation as a powerful warrior goddess in response to the threat posed by Mahishasura underscores the idea that divine intervention can arise to combat evil and restore balance. This narrative serves as an inspiration for devotees, encouraging them to face their own challenges with courage and determination, knowing that they have the goddess's support and protection.

Vindhyavasini's connection to the natural world is a central aspect of her worship and significance. The mountains, rivers, and forests that form her domain are seen as embodiments of her power and presence. This perspective fosters a deep respect for nature and the environment, encouraging devotees to honor and protect the natural world as an extension of the goddess. The reverence for Vindhyavasini thus extends to a broader ecological consciousness, emphasizing the interconnectedness of all life and the need to live in harmony with the environment.

The cultural expressions of Vindhyavasini's worship are diverse and vibrant. Folk songs, dances, and dramas celebrating her deeds and virtues are an integral part of the local culture. These performances often take place during festivals and special occasions, bringing the community together in a shared celebration of the goddess. The storytelling and artistic representations of Vindhyavasini serve to preserve and transmit the cultural and spiritual heritage associated with her, ensuring that her legacy continues to inspire future generations.

In contemporary times, the worship of Vindhyavasini continues to be a source of spiritual solace and empowerment for many. Her role as a protector and provider resonates with devotees facing the challenges of modern life, offering them a sense of stability and assurance. The goddess's emphasis on strength, resilience, and the protective power of the divine feminine provides a powerful counter-narrative to the often chaotic and uncertain nature of contemporary society.

Vindhyavasini's teachings also emphasize the importance of community and collective worship. The communal rituals and festivals dedicated to the goddess foster a sense of solidarity and shared purpose among devotees. These gatherings provide opportunities for social interaction, mutual support, and the reinforcement of cultural values and traditions. The sense of community that arises from the worship of Vindhyavasini helps to strengthen social bonds and create a supportive and cohesive social fabric.

Furthermore, Vindhyavasini's worship highlights the significance of the feminine divine in Hindu spirituality. As an incarnation of Durga, she embodies the qualities of strength, compassion, and protection that are central to the concept of Shakti, the divine feminine energy. The reverence for Vindhyavasini reflects the broader recognition of the power and importance of the feminine principle in the cosmos. This perspective challenges patriarchal norms and emphasizes the value and dignity of the feminine in both the spiritual and material realms.

Vindhyavasini, the mountain-dwelling goddess, represents the powerful and protective aspects of the divine feminine. Her worship, deeply rooted in the cultural and spiritual traditions of the Vindhya Range, celebrates her role as a warrior, protector, and benefactor. Through her connection to the natural world, Vindhyavasini embodies the strength and resilience of the mountains, offering her devotees a sense of stability and assurance. Her teachings and worship emphasize the importance of resilience, community, and the reverence for nature, providing valuable insights and inspiration for contemporary life. By honoring Vindhyavasini, devotees affirm their connection to the divine, the natural world, and each other, fostering a sense of harmony, strength, and spiritual fulfillment.

"Manasa's story of resilience and devotion
highlights the protective aspects of the divine
feminine. Her worship emphasizes the importance
of healing and renewal. She teaches us to respect the
natural world and its cycles."

TWENTY

TULSI: THE SACRED PLANT AND DIVINE DEVI

Tulsi, the sacred plant and divine Devi, holds an unparalleled place in Hindu culture and spirituality. Revered as a manifestation of the goddess Lakshmi and an embodiment of purity and devotion, Tulsi is not merely a plant but a living symbol of the divine presence in the natural world. The worship of Tulsi reflects a deep ecological consciousness and an understanding of the interconnectedness of all life. Her significance extends beyond religious rituals to encompass various aspects of daily life, health, and environmental stewardship.

Tulsi, also known as Holy Basil (Ocimum sanctum), is considered the queen of herbs in Hindu tradition. Her leaves, stems, and flowers are believed to possess potent medicinal properties, making her an integral part of Ayurvedic medicine. The plant is known for its ability to boost immunity, fight infections, and promote overall well-being. This medicinal value, combined with her spiritual significance, elevates Tulsi to a revered status in Hindu households and temples.

The mythology surrounding Tulsi is rich with stories that highlight her divine nature and the reasons for her veneration. According to one prominent legend, Tulsi was a devoted follower of Vishnu in her previous life. Her unwavering devotion and purity earned her the boon of being eternally associated with the deity. As a result, Tulsi is often depicted as an incarnation of Lakshmi, the goddess of wealth and prosperity, and the consort of Vishnu. This association underscores her role as a provider of spiritual and material benefits to her devotees.

Another significant story involves the demon king Jalandhara, whose wife Vrinda was a devout worshipper of Vishnu. Vrinda's devotion made Jalandhara invincible, and the gods struggled to defeat him. To restore cosmic balance, Vishnu assumed the form of Jalandhara and approached Vrinda, thereby breaking her chastity and weakening the demon. Upon realizing the deception, Vrinda cursed Vishnu to become a black stone (Shaligram), and out of her immense devotion and sorrow, she immolated herself. From her ashes, the Tulsi plant emerged, symbolizing purity, devotion, and sacrifice. This legend highlights Tulsi's association with steadfast devotion and the transformative power of devotion and sacrifice.

The worship of Tulsi is an integral part of Hindu religious practices. In many households, Tulsi is planted in a special altar known as the Tulsi Vrindavan, often located in the courtyard or garden. The Vrindavan is usually a small, decorated structure where the plant is tended with great care and reverence. Daily rituals include watering the plant, lighting a lamp or incense, and offering prayers. These practices underscore the sanctity of Tulsi and her role as a living presence of the divine within the home.

Tulsi Vivah, a ceremonial marriage of the Tulsi plant to Vishnu or his incarnations, is a significant festival celebrated in the Hindu month of Kartik (October-November). This ritual symbolizes the divine union and marks the beginning of the wedding season in India. During the ceremony, the Tulsi plant is adorned with colorful decorations, and devotees perform elaborate rituals to solemnize the marriage. This festival highlights the cultural and spiritual importance of Tulsi, reinforcing her status as a beloved and revered deity.

The environmental significance of Tulsi is profound. As a plant that is easy to grow and maintain, Tulsi is a symbol of ecological sustainability and the importance of caring for the environment. Her worship encourages the planting and nurturing of Tulsi in households and communities, promoting green spaces and contributing to environmental conservation. The reverence for Tulsi reflects a broader understanding of the need to live in harmony with nature and to respect the interconnectedness of all life forms.

The use of Tulsi in Ayurvedic medicine further underscores her importance in promoting health and well-being. Known for her adaptogenic properties, Tulsi helps the body adapt to stress and maintain balance. She is used in various formulations to treat respiratory conditions, digestive issues, and skin disorders. The holistic approach of Ayurveda, which emphasizes the integration of body, mind, and spirit, aligns with the reverence for Tulsi as a sacred plant that nurtures all aspects of well-being.

Tulsi's significance extends to her role in rituals and ceremonies. Her leaves are considered so sacred that they are often used in offerings to deities, especially Vishnu and Krishna. The presence of Tulsi leaves in rituals is believed to purify and sanctify the offerings, enhancing their spiritual efficacy. In many temples, the water used for ablutions (charanamrit) is infused with Tulsi leaves, signifying purification and divine blessing.

The cultural expressions of Tulsi's veneration are diverse and vibrant. In literature, poetry, and folk songs, Tulsi is celebrated as a symbol of purity, devotion, and divine grace. These cultural forms serve to transmit the values and beliefs associated with Tulsi across generations, ensuring the continuity of her worship and the preservation of her legacy. Through these expressions, the story and significance of Tulsi are kept alive, fostering a deep and abiding connection to the sacred plant.

Tulsi's role in promoting community and social cohesion is also significant. The shared practice of tending to the Tulsi plant and participating in communal rituals fosters a sense of unity and collective responsibility. These practices reinforce the values of mutual respect, care for the environment, and the importance of maintaining sacred traditions. The communal aspect of Tulsi worship helps to strengthen social bonds and create a supportive and cohesive community.

In contemporary times, the worship of Tulsi continues to be relevant, reflecting the enduring values of devotion, purity, and ecological consciousness. As environmental concerns become increasingly urgent, the reverence for Tulsi offers a model for sustainable living and environmental stewardship. Her worship encourages individuals and communities to take responsibility for the health of the planet and to cultivate practices that promote ecological balance and sustainability.

The modern relevance of Tulsi also extends to the field of wellness and holistic health. With the growing interest in natural remedies and alternative medicine, Tulsi's medicinal properties are increasingly recognized and valued. The incorporation of Tulsi in wellness practices and health products reflects a broader trend towards integrating traditional knowledge with contemporary approaches to health and well-being. This convergence highlights the timeless wisdom embodied by Tulsi and her role in promoting holistic health.

Tulsi, the sacred plant and divine Devi, represents the profound connection between the divine and the natural world. Her worship reflects a deep reverence for nature, an understanding of the interconnectedness of all life, and the importance of living in harmony with the environment. Through her association with purity, devotion, and health, Tulsi embodies the values of holistic well-being and ecological consciousness. Her significance in Hindu culture and spirituality underscores the timeless wisdom of honoring and nurturing the natural world as a manifestation of the divine. As a living symbol of these values, Tulsi continues to inspire and guide individuals and communities towards a more harmonious and sustainable way of life.

"Bhumi, as the Earth Goddess, symbolizes the nurturing and sustaining aspects of the planet. Her teachings emphasize ecological stewardship and respect for all life forms. She reminds us of our responsibility to protect and honor the Earth."

TWENTY-ONE
SUMMARY

The goddesses of Hindu mythology embody the diverse and dynamic aspects of the divine feminine, each representing unique qualities and powers that contribute to the spiritual and cultural fabric of India. These goddesses, revered and worshipped through various rituals, festivals, and cultural expressions, reflect the profound connection between the divine, nature, and human life. Their stories, symbols, and teachings offer valuable insights into the principles of devotion, strength, resilience, compassion, and ecological consciousness.

Lalita Tripura Sundari, the goddess of bliss and beauty, exemplifies the transformative power of the divine feminine. Her worship, deeply rooted in Tantric practices, emphasizes the pursuit of spiritual bliss and the realization of one's unity with the divine. The Lalita Sahasranama, a sacred text enumerating her thousand names, portrays her as the universal mother and the source of all creation. Lalita's iconography, rituals, and festivals, such as Navaratri, celebrate her role as a warrior and protector, highlighting her strength, grace, and beauty. Through her teachings, Lalita inspires devotees to cultivate inner beauty, grace, and a deep appreciation for the interconnectedness of all life.

Vindhyavasini, the mountain-dwelling goddess, is closely associated with the Vindhya Range in central India. She is revered as an incarnation of Durga, embodying the qualities of strength, courage, and protection. Her story, linked to the battle against the demon Mahishasura, underscores her role as a guardian of cosmic balance and a protector of her devotees. The Vindhyavasini Temple in Uttar Pradesh serves as a major pilgrimage site, where festivals such as Navaratri are celebrated with great devotion. Vindhyavasini's worship reflects a deep respect for nature and the environment, emphasizing the need to live in harmony with the natural world.

Tulsi, the sacred plant and divine Devi, holds a unique place in Hindu culture and spirituality. Revered as a manifestation of Lakshmi and an embodiment of purity and devotion, Tulsi is both a sacred plant and a living symbol of the divine. Her worship involves daily rituals, including the tending of the Tulsi Vrindavan, a special altar in households. Tulsi Vivah, a ceremonial marriage of the Tulsi plant to Vishnu, highlights her cultural and spiritual significance. The medicinal properties of Tulsi, recognized in Ayurvedic medicine, underscore her role in promoting health and well-being. Tulsi's veneration reflects a broader ecological consciousness and the importance of sustainable living.

Gayatri, the personification of the Vedic hymn, embodies the divine light of knowledge and the universal power of the mantra. The Gayatri Mantra, one of the most important hymns in Vedic literature, is a prayer for spiritual awakening and enlightenment. Gayatri's iconography, depicting her as a beautiful goddess with five faces and ten arms, symbolizes her multifaceted nature and her role as the bestower of wisdom. The worship of Gayatri, particularly through the recitation of the Gayatri Mantra, emphasizes the transformative potential of meditation and devotion. Gayatri's teachings promote the values of intellectual and spiritual enlightenment, fostering a deeper understanding of oneself and the universe.

Bhumi, the Earth Goddess, represents the nurturing and sustaining aspects of the Earth. As the personification of the planet, Bhumi embodies qualities of fertility, stability, and nourishment. Her worship highlights the intimate relationship between humans and the natural world, emphasizing the need for ecological stewardship and respect for the environment. Festivals such as Pongal and Makar Sankranti celebrate Bhumi's role in agriculture and the cycles of nature. Bhumi's significance extends to various cultural and literary traditions, where she is celebrated as a symbol of resilience and the interconnectedness of all life.

Manasa, the serpent goddess of fertility and health, holds a unique place in the religious traditions of Bengal and Assam. As a deity associated with snakes, Manasa embodies the protective and potentially dangerous aspects of these creatures. She is revered for her ability to cure snakebites, promote fertility, and bring prosperity and health. Manasa's worship involves rituals and offerings that seek to appease snakes and invoke her protective powers. The Manasa Mangal, a collection of Bengali narrative poems, celebrates her life and deeds, highlighting her role as a compassionate and accessible deity.

Santoshi Mata, the Mother of Satisfaction, is a relatively recent addition to the Hindu pantheon. Her worship gained prominence through the 1975 Bollywood film "Jai Santoshi Maa," which depicted her as a powerful and compassionate goddess. Santoshi Mata is revered for her ability to grant peace, happiness, and contentment. The primary ritual associated with her worship is the Santoshi Mata Vrat, a fast observed on Fridays. This ritual emphasizes the values of patience, perseverance, and devotion, reflecting Santoshi Mata's role as a provider of satisfaction and harmony in familial and personal life.

Kamakhya, the goddess of desire and fertility, is a central figure in the tantric practices of Assam. Her worship is closely associated with the Kamakhya Temple, one of the most important Shakti Peethas. Kamakhya represents the primal forces of nature and the cycles of fertility, and her worship celebrates the sacredness of desire and the feminine body. The Ambubachi Mela, a festival marking Kamakhya's menstruation, underscores her role as a goddess of fertility and the life-giving properties of the Earth. Kamakhya's teachings emphasize the acceptance and transcendence of physical desires as a path to spiritual enlightenment.

Chandi, the fierce form of Shakti, is one of the most formidable goddesses in Hindu mythology. Her story, recounted in the Devi Mahatmya, celebrates her might and valor in battling the forces of darkness. Chandi's battle with the demon Mahishasura highlights her role as a protector and restorer of cosmic balance. Her worship, particularly during Durga Puja, reflects her significance as a warrior goddess. Chandi's teachings emphasize the importance of inner strength and the ability to confront and overcome adversity, promoting the values of resilience and righteous action.

Vindhyavasini, the mountain-dwelling goddess, is closely associated with the Vindhya Range in central India. She is revered as an incarnation of Durga, embodying the qualities of strength, courage, and protection. Her story, linked to the battle against the demon Mahishasura, underscores her role as a guardian of cosmic balance and a protector of her devotees. The Vindhyavasini Temple in Uttar Pradesh serves as a major pilgrimage site, where festivals such as Navaratri are celebrated with great devotion. Vindhyavasini's worship reflects a deep respect for nature and the environment, emphasizing the need to live in harmony with the natural world.

Radha, the symbol of divine love, is celebrated for her pure and selfless love for Krishna. Her relationship with Krishna represents the soul's yearning for union with the divine. The stories of Radha and Krishna, filled with enchanting episodes of their divine play in Vrindavan, highlight the intensity and spiritual depth of their love. Radha's devotion to Krishna is marked by intense longing and separation, symbolizing the soul's journey towards spiritual enlightenment. Radha's worship, particularly through devotional songs and dances, emphasizes the values of love, devotion, and spiritual union.

Sita, the embodiment of virtue and devotion, is one of the most revered figures in Hindu mythology. As the consort of Lord Rama, Sita exemplifies the ideals of righteousness and devotion. Her life, marked by trials and tribulations, reflects the virtues of patience, purity, and unwavering dedication to dharma. Sita's story, chronicled in the Ramayana, provides profound insights into the ideals of dharma and the transformative power of devotion. Her unwavering faith, moral integrity, and compassionate nature make her an enduring figure of inspiration and reverence.

Parvati, the gentle mother and nurturer, stands as a symbol of love, devotion, and compassion. As the consort of Lord Shiva and the mother of Ganesha and Kartikeya, Parvati embodies the ideal qualities of womanhood. Her life story, filled with devotion and perseverance, highlights her role as a nurturing and protective mother. Parvati's worship emphasizes the importance of balance, perseverance, and compassion, encouraging individuals to cultivate virtues such as love and resilience.

Kali, the fierce protector and destroyer, represents the darker and more powerful aspects of the divine feminine. As a manifestation of Parvati, Kali embodies the destructive and transformative forces necessary to maintain cosmic balance. Her fearsome appearance, with wild hair, a garland of skulls, and a protruding tongue, symbolizes the raw and untamed energy of the divine. Kali's worship, particularly during festivals like Kali Puja, reflects her role as a protector against evil and a guide through the darker aspects of existence. Her teachings emphasize the importance of embracing one's shadow self and the transformative power of facing fears and challenges.

Saraswati, the goddess of wisdom and learning, is revered as the embodiment of knowledge, music, and the arts. She is often depicted holding a veena (a musical instrument) and a book, symbolizing the integration of artistic and intellectual pursuits. Saraswati's worship, especially during the festival of Vasant Panchami, highlights the importance of education, creativity, and the pursuit of knowledge. Her teachings encourage the development of intellectual and artistic talents, promoting the values of learning and cultural enrichment.

Lakshmi, the bestower of wealth and prosperity, is one of the most widely worshipped goddesses in Hinduism. As the consort of Vishnu, Lakshmi embodies the qualities of abundance, fortune, and beauty. Her presence in households and businesses reflects the desire for prosperity and well-being. The festival of Diwali, dedicated to Lakshmi, is a time for invoking her blessings for wealth and success. Lakshmi's teachings emphasize the importance of gratitude, generosity, and ethical living in the pursuit of prosperity.

Durga, the invincible warrior goddess, is celebrated for her strength, valor, and protective nature. Her story, particularly the battle against Mahishasura, highlights her role as a defender of righteousness and a protector of the cosmos. Durga's worship, especially during Durga Puja, is marked by elaborate rituals, processions, and cultural performances. Her teachings promote the values of courage, resilience, and the importance of standing up against injustice.

The goddesses of Hindu mythology, through their diverse and dynamic manifestations, offer profound insights into the principles of devotion, strength, resilience, compassion, and ecological consciousness. Their worship reflects a deep connection between the divine, nature, and human life, emphasizing the importance of living in harmony with the natural world and cultivating virtues that promote spiritual and material well-being. Through their stories, symbols, and teachings, these goddesses continue to inspire and guide individuals and communities towards a more harmonious, compassionate, and fulfilling existence.

ᐳᐳᐳ

Citation And References

This book represents the culmination of extensive research and meticulous analysis, incorporating a diverse range of sources, including numerous books, scholarly studies, and personal experiences. Additionally, I have scoured various websites to gather relevant information and data essential for the compilation of this work. I have taken every precaution to ensure the accuracy of the information presented and have diligently cited all sources to acknowledge their contributions.

Despite these efforts, the possibility of inadvertent errors remains. I deeply value the insights of my readers and appreciate any feedback that can help identify and rectify such inaccuracies. I encourage you to bring any discrepancies to my attention.

Your feedback is not only welcome but crucial, as it will aid in correcting current editions and enhancing the content of future ones. I am committed to maintaining the highest standards of accuracy and reliability in my work and thank you for your support and understanding.

Additionally, I firmly uphold the principle of freedom of speech and expression as guaranteed under Article 19(1)(a) of the Constitution of India, and I respect the diverse viewpoints and expressions of all readers.

ϷϷϷ

Other Books Of The Author

1. Empowering Minds: A Journey into Women's Self-Discovery and Power
2. The Dynamics of Motivation: Catalyzing Thought into Action
3. Meditation and Mental Well Being: The Path to Inner Peace and Clarity
4. The Psychology of Child Education: Nurturing Future Generations
5. Ethical Enlightenment: A Modern Guide to Living with Integrity
6. Voices of Empowerment: Stories of Women Rising Against Odds
7. Social Psychology in Everyday Life: Understanding Human Connections
8. The Essence of Motivational Speaking: Inspiring Change in Others
9. Balancing Acts: Women, Work, and the Will to Lead
10. Guiding with Grace: Raising Children with Compassion and Awareness
11. The Power of Positive Aging: Embracing Life After Fifty
12. Building Resilient Communities: Social Work in Action
13. The Ethical Educator: Principles for Teaching and Learning
14. From Insight to Impact: Social Psychology for a Better World
15. The Ethics of Empathy: A Guide to Ethical Living
16. The Science of Empowering the Self: Navigating Life's Challenges with Psychological Wisdom
17. The Mindful Conscious Leader: Meditation Techniques for Modern Management
18. Pioneering Spirit: Women's Pathways to Leadership and Empowerment
19. Feeling to Healing: The Role of Emotional Intelligence in Child Development
20. Transformative Talks and Words of Inspiration: Insights into Motivational Oratory

Bhajan

101. Pilgrimage of the Soul: Spiritual Journeys in India

❧❧❧

Contact

Dr. Minakshi Bansal
Social Activist
Ahmedabad, Gujarat, Bharat
minakshiindiag20@yahoo.com

❦❦❦

|| LOKAHA SAMASTHAHA SUKHINO BHAVANTU ||